Scott, I appreciate your friendship & partnership in the Gospel!

Rev 22:4

[illegible]

REVELATION

God's Final Word

What the Last Book in the Bible Reveals about the Future

DAVID O. DYKES

For a complete list of books and broadcast messages by Dr. David O. Dykes available in print, CD/Cassette or VHS/DVD, please visit the Discover Life online Resource Center at www.discoverlife.tv. Call toll-free 24 hours a day (888) 539-LIFE (5433).

Green Acres Baptist Church
1607 Troup Highway
Tyler, Texas 75701
www.gabc.org

Produced with the assistance of Fluency Organization, Inc. in Tyler, TX.

Also by David O. Dykes

Do Angels Really Exist?

Handling Life's Disappointments

Character out of Chaos: Daring to be a Daniel in Today's World

Ten Requirements for America's Survival

Angels Really Do Exist: Signs of Heaven on Earth

Finding Peace in Your Pain

No, That's NOT in the Bible

This book is lovingly dedicated to the members of Green Acres Baptist Church in Tyler, Texas.

They are the greatest congregation on the planet, and I am humbly grateful for their constant prayers, encouragement and freedom to study and teach God's Word here and around the world.

Table of Contents

From the Author

No doubt, people are fascinated with the book of Revelation. Many people begin reading the Bible at Revelation, but this is a serious mistake. This book plunges the reader into a confusing array of dragons, trumpets, bowls and seals. A person starting here might well set aside the whole Bible in frustration, thinking the rest of it is as difficult to decipher.

It is no accident that God placed Revelation as the last book of the Bible. If you have read the rest of the Bible before you come to Revelation, you will be much better equipped to understand it because it is the climax of the entire revelation of God to his people.

One of my spiritual mentors, C.S. Lewis, wrote:

> "When the author walks on to the stage the play is over. God is going to invade, alright, but what is the good of saying you are on His side then, when you see the whole natural universe melting away like a dream and something else—something it never entered your head to conceive—comes crashing in; something so beautiful to some of us and so terrible to others that none of us will have any choice left? For this time it will be God without disguise; something so

> overwhelming that it will strike either irresistible love or irresistible horror into every creature.
>
> It will be too late then to choose your side. There is no use saying you choose to lie down when it has become impossible to stand up. That will not be the time for choosing; it will be the time when we discover which side we really have chosen, whether we realized it before or not.
>
> Now, today, this moment, is our chance to choose the right side. God is holding back to give us that chance. It will not last forever. We must take it or leave it."
>
> (from *Mere Christianity*)

I wrote this book to help you study this book and unravel its mystery so you can plainly see in simple language what it means. Revelation will strengthen you to wait patiently, to work diligently and to obey faithfully as you anticipate Christ's appearing. Contrary to what some may think, Revelation is a book of extreme optimism. Although it paints a dark picture of God's judgment against sin, it doesn't stop there—it looks beyond to the final victory of God, which is even more certain than tomorrow's sunrise!

May you be blessed as you allow God's Word to saturate your soul!

David O. Dykes
October 25, 2010

Introduction

There is a marvelous unity to the Word of God that begins with the book of Genesis and ends with the book of Revelation. Revelation is the last book in the Bible, but it shares much in common with the first book where the Story all starts. Even though they were written thousands of years apart, Genesis and Revelation are actually sister books.

- In Genesis, God created the heavens and the earth. In Revelation, the first heaven and the first earth pass away and a new heaven and a new earth arrive.
- In Genesis, we read about Paradise lost when Adam and Eve chose to sin. In Revelation, we see Paradise restored at an undisclosed time in the future for those who know and love God.
- In Genesis, humanity is driven from the Tree of the Knowledge of Good and Evil because of sin, and God even stations cherubim there to guard the entrance to the Garden of Eden. In Revelation, God himself welcomes his children to eat and drink at the foot of the Tree of Life.
- In Genesis, Satan slithers his way to a grand entrance. In Revelation, we celebrate his terrible, long-awaited exit.
- In Genesis, Satan's doom is pronounced. In Revelation, Satan's doom is fulfilled.

- In Genesis, we read about the first Adam's wife, Eve. In Revelation, the focus is on the second Adam (Jesus) and his Bride, the Church.
- In Genesis, we see the first tears to grace a human cheekbone when Adam and Eve were cursed because of sin. In Revelation, God wipes the last tears from our eyes.
- In Genesis, Adam and Eve are separated from God. In Revelation, we are in God's presence forevermore.
- In Genesis, Cain and Abel experience the first murder and the first physical death. In Revelation, there will be no more death and dying.

What Adam messed up, Jesus Christ fixed up. The story of humanity wrapped within the pages of the Bible is a history of being formed, being deformed by sin and then being transformed by Jesus Christ.

Interestingly, Genesis and Revelation are the two most attacked books of the Bible. Many people will tell you the book of Genesis is nothing but a myth. And some insist the book of Revelation is only a mystery. One book you can't believe, and the other is so complicated you can't understand it.

Dr. Vance Havner countered this argument with humor when he said, "If the book of Genesis is a myth, I am myth-taken and myth-understood and I'm myth-tified." Likewise, Dr. R.G. Lee raised the stakes and said, "If the Bible is a myth, then a canary bird can fly across the Atlantic Ocean with the Washington Monument tied to its tail." The Bible is much more relevant than any newspaper and more accurate than any science book we have today. My goal in writing this book on Revelation is to show everyone how to easily understand it and apply the truth to his or her life.

So, let's start from the beginning and unravel the truth to this mysterious book, chapter by chapter. You'll notice I've divided this book into chapter numbers that correspond with the chapters in Revelation. Some chapters are short, and some are long; some have more information in them than others do. This format allows you to use this book in a small group setting and discuss each chapter. It will also help you "keep your place" in the storyline and provide you with an easy-to-use study resource.

What Revelation Means

The full title of Revelation is, "The Revelation of Jesus Christ." If you have access to a King James Version of the Bible, the chapter heading probably says something like, "The Revelation of St. John the Divine," referring to John, the disciple, who wrote it. You realize, of course, the titles of books are not inspired by God—some scribe just added that subheading for clarification later. In fact, chapter and verse divisions were not in the original language either. They were added centuries later. The real title of the book comes from the first verse, in the first chapter:

> The revelation of Jesus Christ which God gave him to show his servants what must soon take place. He made it known by sending his angel to his servant, John who testifies to everything he saw— that is, the word of God and the testimony of Jesus Christ. Blessed is the one who reads the words of this prophecy, and blessed are those who hear it and take to heart what is written in it because the time is near. (Revelation 1:1-3)

One of my pet peeves is when well-meaning people mistakenly call this book, "Revelations"—using the plural form of the word. You'll never make that mistake again when you realize what the word means. The word, *revelation,* is the word, *apokalupsis*, where we get our word, "apocalypse." It's a word that means *to unveil* or *to unwrap.* Imagine that a city commissioned an artist to sculpt a beautiful statue for the front of a public building. They wanted the artist to work without people seeing his progress, so the city covered the area with a large canvas. After a few months, the time finally came for the unveiling. The crowd gathered and the band played. At the given signal, someone pulled a rope, the canvas fell off and the statue was finally "*apokalupsis.*" It was "revealed" for all to see. That's what that word, *revelation* means. It is the unveiling of Jesus Christ.

If, on the other hand, you are more interested in the book of Revelation because you want to know exactly what's going to happen in the future, you won't necessarily be rewarded. That's not the overarching purpose of the book. Its purpose is to reveal Jesus Christ to you. That's the whole point. Every book in the Bible is about Jesus, but this book specifically says its intent is to *reveal* Jesus Christ.

Whose Letter Is It?

Let's look at another angle of this book. To whom was Revelation written? According to Revelation 1, this book was originally a letter given to the servants of Jesus Christ. It's not given to fortunetellers and those who call themselves modern prophets, desperately trying to predict the future. They are what I call "prophecy junkies." They don't necessarily want to read more about Jesus; they just want to predict the future. Non-believers try to study the book of Revelation to find out what's going to happen in the future, but they don't fully understand it. Hollywood tries to make scary movies where evil characters with scary voices read obscure passages from Revelation. But it's not written to them; they're reading somebody else's mail. That consumer approach and attitude will never be rewarded; only those who want to know more about Jesus get to the real truths of this book.

Why Was It Written?

Look again at the opening lines of Revelation. Why was it written? "...to show [Jesus'] servants what must soon take place." Wait a minute. When was this book written? About 90A.D. It's almost 2,000 years later and these events haven't happened yet; why does the Bible say it will "soon" take place? That use of the word "soon" is translated to mean "whenever it begins, it will occur with great rapidity"! When the cycle described here is set in motion, it will all take place quickly. In other words, things are coming to a head.

I happen to believe with all my heart that we are living in a time when the cycle could start at any moment. Why? There are many reasons, but the primary reason is because of Israel. Revelation says a lot about the nation of Israel. In 70A.D., the nation of Israel as we know it was wiped off the face of the earth by the Romans and did not become a nation again until midway through the 20th century. Before that time, it was completely impossible to understand these specific references to Israel in Revelation. If scholars tried to interpret these references, they often mistakenly interpreted Israel as "the Church." When Israel was officially recognized as a nation in 1948, that set the stage for the events described in Revelation to happen relatively quickly from that time forward.

Symbolism in Revelation

It's important to recognize the purpose of Revelation and the audience for whom it was written. Another introductory key to understanding this book is to realize that it is a book of symbols. Some people say, "You can't take the Bible literally. You have to take the Bible symbolically." There's a word for that—*baloney!* Sure, there is symbolism in the Bible, and Revelation is full of symbols. However, we must look for the literal truth behind the symbols. For example, one of the symbols in Revelation is a red dragon with seven heads. What is that? That sounds like something you would dream after eating raw cabbage and ice cream, riding a roller coaster and sleeping on a waterbed—a bad nightmare. Do I believe there is such a thing as a red dragon? No, it is a symbol, and the Bible explains most of the symbols used in Revelation. John identifies this dragon:

> The great dragon was hurled down, that ancient serpent called the devil, or Satan, who leads the whole world astray. He was hurled to the earth, and his angels with him. (Revelation 12:9)

The symbol is a dragon; the reality is Satan, himself. All of the symbols in Revelation are powerful.

Let's say a thousand years from now archeologists are digging in the ancient ruins of what was once called Texas. They find remnants of a newspaper dated from November 1992. On the paper is a large drawing of a donkey with a baseball bat hitting an elephant on the head. If you don't know the symbols, it doesn't make sense. One archeologist says, "I know what that means. Back in ancient Texas, they used to have a circus act with a donkey who would beat up elephants." Another archeologist shakes his head and says, "No, I don't think so. Baseball was a popular game in ancient Texas. Back in 1992, the Donkeys beat the Elephants in the World Series." Both of them would be wrong! However, the third archaeologist has studied the symbols of American history. He accurately identifies the symbols of the Democratic and Republican parties and recalls that in the 1992 presidential election the Democrats defeated the Republicans. Knowing what the symbols mean helps uncover the truth. That's why we must understand the book of Revelation in light of what the symbols mean. Now that you have some of the keys to understanding Revelation, let's look at how the storyline of Revelation unfolds.

John Wrote Revelation

John "saw" everything in this book as a vision and wrote about what he witnessed in three parts. The key to understanding the whole book of Revelation is in 1:19; it explains how Jesus wanted John to write this vision in thirds. Jesus told him to: "Write, therefore, what you have seen, what is now and what will take place later." There are three parts of this instruction: 1) Write what you have just seen (the vision of Jesus Christ coming to him); 2) Write what is now (what's happening regarding the seven churches in Revelation) and; 3) Write what will take place (future events). These sections serve as a table of contents for the entire book. Let's look at that first part—what John just saw.

Part One: What You Have Seen

Here's John, minding his own business and worshiping the Lord on the Lord's Day (Sunday), when suddenly he heard a voice behind him—it was Jesus! Chapter 1 of Revelation is the only physical description of Jesus' appearance found in the Bible. This first part Jesus told him to write is just a brief section of the book and covers chapter 1:1-20 only. Jesus says in effect, "What did you just see when I came to you, John? Write it down." And John does.

Part Two: What Is Now

In chapters 2 and 3 of Revelation, John describes the second section of what Jesus told him to write: "…what is now." According to 1:4, Revelation was originally written as a letter addressed to seven churches in different ancient locations: Ephesus, Smyrna, Pergamum, Thyatira, Sardis, Philadelphia and Laodicea. They were actual churches during the time John lived. However, these churches also represent all churches and all Christians of all time, including today. This second section to the churches is short, covering just chapters 2 and 3. The bulk of Revelation is about the third section, which we call "the future."

Part Three: What Will Take Place Later

Beginning with chapter 4:1 all the way through the end of the book, the subject is the future. This is the third part of what Jesus says in 1:19 for John to write: "…what will take place later." John says at the beginning of chapter 4:

> After this I looked, and there before me was a door standing open in heaven. And the voice I had first heard speaking to me like a trumpet said,

> "Come up here, and I will show you *what must take place after this*." Revelation 4:1

These are the same words in Greek as used in 1:19: "…what will take place later." What's going to happen later? I can summarize five key events that have yet to happen, as described in Revelation, and they are biggies.

1. The Rapture

At the Rapture of the Church, Jesus comes back in the clouds and Christians are caught up to be with the Lord in the air. Some people believe Christians are going to be on earth during the time of the Tribulation. I don't agree. Notice that in the first three chapters in Revelation, the emphasis is on the Church, the Church, the Church. Then in chapter 4:1—whoosh! We're out of here! The word "church" is never mentioned again until the last chapter after the creation of the new heavens and earth. Why is the Church dropped from the storyline? Because we have been raptured and are no longer living on the earth.

2. The Tribulation

The Bible describes this as a seven-year period of time when people of the earth hate God and rebel against him. One charismatic person called the Antichrist will come on the scene as a world leader to provide peace to the nations. It has never before been technologically possible for one world leader to arise…until now. Advancements in communication technology have enabled us to watch a war in real time and talk live via satellite feed with almost anyone in the world. Our culture is abuzz with the "New World Order," one world economy and one worldwide monetary system. It's all building toward this idea of a one-world government led by one man—the Antichrist.

3. The Final Battle

At the end of the seven-year period of Tribulation, Jesus Christ is going to come back with the saints for a great battle. Remember, at the rapture of the Church, Jesus comes back in the clouds and Christians are caught up to be with the Lord in the air. However, at the Final Battle, he will return to earth as a warrior prepared for battle. And guess what? We saddle up with him and join him for the fight! Martin Luther wrote the famous hymn, "A Mighty Fortress Is Our God," about how one little word is capable of taking Satan down for the count. At this final battle, the most lethal weapon is the Word of God.

4. The Millennium

The Bible teaches that when Jesus comes back and wins the Final Battle, he is going to set up an earthly kingdom for a thousand years, and we will reign with him. In Revelation 20:4-6, John talks three times about reigning with Christ one thousand years. The world will experience an unparalleled time of perfect peace and prosperity when all the nations will come before Jesus.

5. Paradise for Eternity

The final event on God's prophetic calendar is our experience of Paradise for all eternity, as described in the final chapters of Revelation. God says, "No longer will there be any curse" (Revelation 22:3). Do you know what the last word in the Old Testament is? *Curse*. That's the story of the whole Old Testament: the curse brought on by sin. In the last chapter of the Bible, it says:

> No longer will there be any curse. The throne of God and of the land will be in the city and the servants will serve him. They will see his face and his name will be on their foreheads. There will be no more night. They will not need the light of a lamp nor the light of the sun for the Lord God will give them light. They will reign forever and ever! (Revelation 22:3-5)

The End of Revelation

There is also a warning posted at the end of this book in 22:18 where Jesus says, "I warn everyone who hears the words of the prophecy of this book: If anyone adds anything to them, God will add to him the plagues described in this book." If you're the least bit familiar with any of the terrible plagues described in Revelation, you realize that's the last thing you would want to happen to you!

It's a very dangerous practice to add to the words of Scripture. In fact, if we alter or add to God's Word, he will take something away from us. He says, "And if anyone takes words away from this book of prophecy, God will take away from him his share in the tree of life and in the holy city, which are described in this book" (22:19).

When you study Revelation, you might be tempted to skip over parts of it—especially parts that are hard to decipher. But there is a blessing waiting for the student who studies it in its entirety.

CHAPTER 1

An Unexpected Voice

Revelation is the only book in the Bible with a blessing promised to everyone who reads and applies what they learn here. Revelation 1:3 says, "Blessed is the one who reads the words of this prophecy and blessed are those who hear it and take to heart what is written in it, because the time is near." It's always good to study and apply God's Word, but the Bible says you are in for a special blessing when you study Revelation.

The Man with a Vision

You may notice something unusual about the salutation to this prophetic book. A salutation is a greeting or a message from the writer to the recipient. In Bible days, they put the name of the letter writer first. This is why 1:4 says John's name first, instead of "Dear so-and-so."

The first character we meet in Revelation is the book's author, John. Tradition says John was the youngest of the disciples and perhaps the closest earthly friend to Jesus. When they were at the Last Supper, the Bible says John was reclining against the chest of Jesus. They were that close.

Tradition tells us all of the disciples died a martyr's death except for John, who was persecuted under the Roman emperor, Domitian. The Roman emperors had colossal egos, and Domitian was one of the first ones who enforced a Roman law requiring every citizen to burn incense to him once a year as Lord of the Universe. John refused and was to be publicly executed for his faith by boiling in oil. However, tradition says they threw the apostle in a vat of hot, gurgling oil, but he didn't die. He was terribly burned and disfigured, but it did not kill him. Under the law, if the Romans were unsuccessful in executing someone, they couldn't try again. Instead, John was exiled to the little island of Patmos in the Mediterranean Sea where he eventually died of natural causes. While John was living on this island as a recluse, he encountered Jesus Christ, who told him to write this Revelation.

Special Delivery for Seven Churches

Revelation was originally written as a letter. Who are the ones receiving this letter of prophecy? Chapter two reveals they are seven ancient churches throughout Asia Minor: Ephesus, Smyrna, Pergamum, Thyatira, Sardis, Philadelphia, and the church in Laodicea.

When you think of churches, don't think of buildings. The early churches did not have buildings, as we do today. These were simple groups of baptized believers meeting together in people's homes. These churches were literal congregations, but they also represent all churches and all Christians of all time. To understand why that's true, we have to unpack the meaning behind our first symbol—the number seven.

Jews assigned meaning to most numbers, a practice known as Gematria. To the Jews, the number *one* was the number of "unity." There are three members of the Trinity, but only one God. The number *two* was the number for "witness." In Jewish law, a fact had to be established by two witnesses or more for it to be true. In Revelation, we are going to be introduced to two key witnesses in the future. The number *three* was the "divine" number: God the Father, God the Son, God the Holy Spirit. The four living creatures in heaven never stop crying out before the throne of God: "Holy, Holy, Holy" (Revelation 4:8), referring to the number of the Trinity.

The number *four* was the number of our planet, the earth. Winds come from the four directions, just as there are four points on the compass. The number *five* was "the Law"—there are five books in the Torah. *Six* was man's number, because man was created on the sixth day. We're going to see later in Revelation where the number *six* has special meaning.

The number *seven* means completion or "a unit." We see several key biblical elements in sets of seven in Revelation. There are seven spirits surrounding the throne of God, for example (Revelation 4:5). Does that mean there are seven Holy Spirits? No, it is a symbolic reference to the unified, singular spirit of God: the Holy Spirit. There are seven wax seals on a scroll, seven trumpets and seven bowls of wrath in Revelation. There are also seven prominent characters in the book of Revelation. And there are seven "new things to come" that God promises at the end of Revelation.

Therefore, when Jesus addresses seven churches in the first few chapters of Revelation, the symmetry of the number "seven" is not by accident. These churches symbolize the totality of all Christians everywhere as a unit. There is one Body of Christ, which is the Church.

"Dispensationalism" takes a little different angle on all of this and teaches that the seven churches represent seven church "ages" or periods of time. For instance, one might pinpoint the characteristics describing one of the seven churches and say, “We are living in the age of the Laodicean church.” I personally don’t believe that teaching. One can find a full spectrum of believers who are like all seven churches: some are like the Laodicean Christians, some are like Ephesian Christians and some are more like the Philadelphian Christians. What Jesus says to all of these churches is an important message to us today.

Descriptions of Jesus

John used a very common greeting followed by a reference to the writer of the letter. It’s a reference to the Trinity: Father, Son and Holy Spirit. “From him who is, and who was, and who is to come and from the seven spirits” (1:4). In other words, this message is from God himself, given to John personally through an encounter with Jesus. Revelation is all about Jesus. There are more designations and descriptions of Jesus here than in any other book of the Bible. This first chapter reveals so much about him, even in the opening verses. He says he is “the faithful witness,” the “firstborn from the dead” and the “ruler” (1:5).

In verses 7 and 8, John gives us a condensed preview of the rest of the book: Jesus is coming back. There are some passages in the Bible indicating that when Jesus comes back he’s going to come “as a thief in the night.” Like a thief, he will slip in suddenly, silently, secretly and then be gone. So why is John talking about him coming in power and majesty when “every eye will see” (1:7)? Is Jesus coming back like a thief in the night? Or a ruler in glory for all to see? Which one is it? The short answer is, “Yes!”

When Jesus comes to rapture the Church, it will be like a

thief in the night—suddenly. This is when we are changed and meet up with Jesus in the clouds. Paul says in 1 Corinthians 15:52 this will happen in a "flash." However, when he comes back seven years later at the Final Battle, "every eye is going to see him." The rapture of the Church will be sudden and secretive, but Christ's return described in Revelation 19 will be an event witnessed by the whole world.

Jesus is Everything

In 1:8, Jesus adds to what John says and gives us more powerful descriptions of his character. But he could have just stopped with the words, "I am…" In Exodus 3, Moses stood at the burning bush and God told him to tell Pharaoh to let his people go. When Moses asked in what name he should make this demand, God said, "You just tell them that my name is 'I AM.'" In the Hebrew language, there is no sense of past, future and present tense. When God said to Moses, "I AM," he was saying, "I have always been. I AM being right now and I will always be!"

That's why Jesus says of himself, "I am the Alpha and the Omega." In the Greek alphabet, alpha is the first letter; omega is the last letter. In our alphabet, he is the A and the Z and everything in between. He is also beyond the scope of time. Jesus is the One "who is, and who was, and who is to come" (1:8). He is the past; he is the present; and he is the future. The Bible says his words are eternal and they will never pass away. There are only two eternal things in this world: the Word of God and the souls of men and women. Your houses, your bank accounts, your cars—everything else is temporary.

When I was studying in seminary in Louisville, Kentucky, I often attended St. Matthews Baptist Church. One wintry

Saturday night, some teenagers broke into the church and stole the audio equipment. Then they set the church on fire. It was in the middle of the night and the church was already consumed in flames when an alarm finally reached the Louisville Fire Department. By the time the firemen got there, the building was almost completely destroyed. I heard the sirens near the church and went to see what had happened. It was so cold that when the firefighters aimed at the flames, the water froze instantly on the parking lot.

The people who had not heard about the fire arrived for church the next morning, only to see their building was nothing but a charred, ice-covered ruin. When they found another place to worship a week later, the pastor talked about his entire personal library being destroyed except for one book. He held up the book they managed to salvage. It was his Bible. Every other book in his office burned to ashes, but not the Word of God. It was a vivid reminder that the Word of God endures forever.

A Sudden Surprise

I've seen the island of Patmos where John wrote this letter, and it is not Gilligan's island with coconuts and beautiful foliage everywhere. It is a barren, windswept sand spit 23 miles southwest of Ephesus in the Aegean Sea. Why did Domitian put John there? To shut him off from the rest of the world so he couldn't preach. However, God always has the last word, doesn't he? While John was on this island, he received a vision from the Lord that would be shared with all Christians everywhere.

Verse 1:10 says this vision happened "on the Lord's Day."

This is the first time the phrase "Lord's Day" is found in the Bible. We assume it is on Sunday. The Jews observed the Sabbath on Saturday. The Lord's Day (Sunday, the First Day) is when Christians gather and worship today, but we are not required to obey the Old Testament Sabbath laws.

John says, "I was in the Spirit," meaning he was praying in the Spirit. He was praying so intently that he was almost carried away in his prayer. Suddenly, he heard a voice "like a trumpet" behind him (1:10). There are many similes in this passage. It wasn't a literal trumpet that John heard; it was a voice *like* a trumpet.

An Unexpected Voice

Have you ever heard God speak to you? Very seldom have I ever sensed what I thought was God actually speaking to me (except through the Bible). I do remember a time when I was a lifeguard at Shako Springs Baptist Assembly between my junior and senior year of high school. I didn't go to that camp to do business with God. I went because I could get a good suntan and meet plenty of girls! However, on the evening of July 24, 1970, I was seated about halfway back in the church auditorium. I don't even remember the name of the preacher who was preaching, but he said God called him to preach when he was seventeen, and he'd been doing that ever since. When he said that, as clear as I have ever heard anything in my life, I heard, "David, that's what I want you to do." You ask, "Was it an audible voice?" No. It was a lot louder than that! I jerked my head around in the pew to see who had said that. No one was there, but I felt God had spoken to my heart.

I know what John is talking about here, and some of you do too! When John turned around, he saw someone standing there. His description of Jesus is stunning, and it's one of the few descriptions we have in the Bible of Jesus' appearance.

What Does Jesus Look Like?

Have you seen the paintings of Jesus with long brown hair, fair skin and big blue eyes? I have been to Israel many times, and I've never met a Jew who looked like that! Sometimes we think Jesus was handsome and dashing when he was on the earth, but the Bible says just the opposite. The Old Testament indicates there was nothing about him that would cause us to look twice at him (Isaiah 53:2). While there was nothing physically attractive about him then, the Bible indicates there was something about his post-resurrection appearance that changed. Sometimes his disciples recognized him, and sometimes they did not. Mark 16:12 says he "appeared in a different form." He also had the ability to suddenly appear among them like a ghost (Luke 24:36-43).

The emphasis on Jesus in the Bible is not his earthly appearance. The best descriptions are of his post-ascension appearance, after he returned to heaven where he is right now. When we see Jesus someday, we're going to see what he looks like as the ascended Christ, the Son of God. This is how Jesus appeared to John on the island of Patmos—and it nearly frightened him to death! When we see Jesus one day either when we die or at the Rapture, he will look more like how John described him.

> I turned around to see the voice that was speaking to me. And when I turned I saw seven golden lampstands, and among the lampstands was someone "like a son of man", dressed in a robe reaching down to his feet and a golden sash around his chest. His head and hair were white like wool, as white as snow, and his eyes were like blazing fire. His feet were like bronze glowing in a furnace, and his voice was like the sound of rushing waters. In his right hand he held seven stars, and out of his mouth came a sharp double-edged sword. His face was like the sun shining in all its brilliance.
>
> When I saw him, I fell at his feet as though dead. Then he placed his right hand on me and said: "Do not be afraid. I am the First and the Last. I am the Living One; I was dead; and behold I am alive for ever and ever! And I hold the keys of death and Hades. Write, therefore, what you have seen, what is now, and what will take place later." (Revelation 1:12-19)

Notice how he describes the way Jesus was dressed—a robe reaching down to his feet. A priest was the only one who kept his feet covered with his robe. This is significant because it is a picture of the priestly role of Jesus, mediating between people and God. John also mentions a golden sash across his chest, the sign of a judge in ancient times. Jesus, the ultimate priest and judge, is standing among the golden lampstands, which represent the seven churches—another reminder that Jesus is in the midst of our churches today.

Also, notice his hair and his head are white like wool, as white as snow. This, too, is symbolic and represents Jesus' wisdom, holiness and purity. Next, notice his eyes—like a "blazing fire." Once more, John is using similes to compare two objects. John didn't say his eyes were on fire; they just reminded him of the intensity of fire. Have you ever met someone who had such an intense look it was as if they had fire in their eyes?

The Bible says we will all appear before the judgment seat of Christ, and his eyes will meet ours. First Corinthians 3:13-15 says our works are going to be judged by fire and "the fire will test the quality of each man's work." It will burn up all the wood, hay and stubble—the worthless things we've done with our lives. But that same fire will purify the gold, silver and precious stones—everything we did in our time on earth that has eternal value. Could it be that all Jesus has to do is just look at us and the fire in his eyes will try our works?

Next, John describes his feet as being like bronze, glowing in a furnace (1:15). His stance as the ultimate Judge is white hot—firm and secure. In his right hand there were seven stars, which we learn in 1:20 represent the seven "angels" or messengers of the seven churches. Who are the messengers? The word *angelos*, translated *angel*, can also mean human messenger. In this context, the seven angels are the pastors of the churches.

John compares his mouth to a two-edged sword. When Jesus spoke, his words cut in both directions to the core of the issue. That's what the Bible says in Hebrews 4:12, "The word of God is quick and powerful and sharper than any two-edged sword." Later in Revelation 19, the only weapon used at the climatic battle at the end of time is this same two-edged sword that comes out of the mouth of the Lamb, Jesus Christ.

His face is described as brilliant radiance in verse 16, bright as the sun. What happened to the apostle Paul in Acts 9 when he was on his way to Damascus and saw Jesus? He describes two things that are parallel with John's description of Christ. First, Paul said there was such a bright light that he couldn't even look at it—a light brighter than the midday sun.

Then he said there was a voice that sounded like thunder; it was such a loud sound he fell to the ground. When this strong and steady Judge spoke, his voice was like a "mighty waterfall." Have ever been to Niagara Falls? I understand you can hear it long before you ever see it because the noise of the cascading water is so loud.

Before I studied this passage of Scripture, I imagined one day entering heaven and giving Jesus a big bear hug. Then I would pull back and look into his eyes and say, "Jesus, I am so glad that I am here now!" That's *not* how it's going to go down! That would be kind of like looking straight into the noonday sun and trying to wrap your arms around it. Jesus' glory, what the Bible calls his "Shekinah" glory, has to be veiled or it would literally kill us. I think when we first see King Jesus, our reaction is going to be much more like John's reaction.

A Surprising Reaction to Jesus

When Jesus died on the cross, he looked down at John, the only disciple (as far as we know) who had the courage to stand at the cross. Jesus had such a close relationship with John that he asked John to take care of his mother after he died. Tradition tells us John was only in his early twenties when Jesus called him. We can date the book of Revelation to about 90A.D., so it had been about 60 years since John had last seen Jesus and he was now an old man. How do you think John reacted after all those years when he saw his Lord, the one he has been preaching about, the one he has been praying to?

I kind of pictured that reunion with Jesus would be like one of those shampoo commercials. You know, the ones where two people are out in a field and they run toward each other in slow motion? The music is playing and their freshly shampooed hair is bouncing all the way. Then, finally, they meet each other in an embrace and start spinning around and around as the music crescendos.

That's how I envisioned Jesus and John would get back together. Wrong!

John says that he fell down "as though dead" when he saw Jesus. If you don't think Jesus is the holy God now, you will when you see him in person! If you think you're going to slip up to him and give him a high five and say, "Man, I'm so glad to see you, Jesus!" you're mistaken.

I imagine I will react the same way John did and fall at his feet. We're going to sink to our knees because of the unbearable glory, holiness and majesty of Jesus. In fact, John doesn't even identify Jesus by name so far. The text seems to indicate that John was so taken aback he must have wondered, "Who is this? It doesn't look like the Jesus that I knew and loved." However, when Jesus started speaking and shared his message with John, he knew it was his Lord.

What Jesus Said to John

First, there was a word of comfort—right when John needed it the most. Picture him at the feet of Jesus, as a dead man, and see Jesus reaching out his right hand, touching him and saying, "Fear not." I love that. It's the same pattern Jesus used throughout his ministry: touching hurting people and saying, "Don't be afraid." Read through the four gospels (Matthew, Mark, Luke and John) sometime and see how many times Jesus reached out his hand and told somebody, "Don't be afraid."

I imagine when he heard those familiar words, John remembered all the times he'd been afraid. Maybe he thought of the time they were on the Sea of Galilee in the midst of a terrible storm. Jesus spoke those very words of comfort and calmed the raging waves. Or maybe John recalled the time they were on their way to the home of Jairus when news arrived that his sick daughter was already dead. Jesus caught Jairus at the edge of despair and said, "Don't be afraid—it's going to be okay." And it was.

How many times does Jesus say, "Don't be afraid?" As many times as you are afraid. Maybe those are the words you most long to hear right now in the midst of your loneliness and confusion. Jesus wants to reach out and touch you, just as he did John, and say, "Don't be afraid." How do we know this is true? Because of who he is. This is the first message in the first chapter of Revelation that we must not miss. Jesus wants us to know him. He tells us: "I am the First and the Last. I am the Living One; I was dead, and behold I am alive for ever and ever! And I hold the keys of death and Hades" 1:17-18. He is the Living One—not even death can hold him down. When we feel our lives are spinning out of control, he is holding it all together. When we are in crisis, he is in control.

Write It Down

The second part of Jesus' opening message to John was a command. He commissions John to write down everything that he is about to see, hear and experience through the rest of the book. Revelation was not John's idea; Jesus told him to write everything down. I will keep referring to 1:19 as the Table of Contents for Revelation because it divides the book into three sections that John is to write: what he has just seen; what is now; and what is to come.

What he has "just seen" was Jesus, and he wrote about the encounter in detail. Now, we come to the second section he is supposed to write: what's happening "now." What follows is a series of letters to seven churches—don't skip this part of Revelation because in every letter to these ancient churches there is a timeless truth for us today. These seven churches represent all churches, of all ages, but when we talk about "churches," we are also talking about individual Christians. What he said to a congregation in 90 A.D., he is saying to you right now—so listen up.

CHAPTER 2

For All Christians of All Times

Where would you look if I told you to open the Bible to 2 Ephesians? You might be looking a long time before you found it—unless you turned to the second chapter in Revelation. The apostle Paul wrote a letter around 63 A.D. to the church at Ephesus where he encouraged them that they might abound in love. About 30 years later, Jesus himself writes another letter to the same church at Ephesus, and we find it right here in Revelation 2. This vibrant congregation of new Christians had somehow lost the flame and excitement for their "first love," Jesus Christ.

Who is the letter from? Jesus is very clear that the letter is not from John; it is from him. He is the "one who walks among the seven golden lampstands." The lampstands represent a church's influence—the city on a hill that cannot be hidden. These were not wax candles as we have today; they were a Middle Eastern type of lamp with a piece of cloth serving as a wick. When Jesus warned the Ephesians, he warned against losing their "lampstand" or influence (2:5).

Jesus' message to all of the churches follows the same pattern. First he points out something good the church is doing—some deed or virtue worth praising. Then he follows that encouragement with a specific area they need to work on, along with a plan for how to correct it. Finally, he gives a warning and a promise. He warns each church what will happen if they do not do what he says, and then he makes a promise to reward their obedience.

For example, in 2:2-3, Jesus pointed out their hard work and perseverance, despite their hardships. They lived in a very secular culture, like Christians living in the middle of Manhattan. Ephesus was one of the three greatest cities of the Roman Empire at the time, next to Rome and Antioch. Ephesus was also the center of a fertility-based pagan religion. Ancient societies tended to worship that which they did not understand. Therefore, many worshiped the mystery of human reproduction and made a religion out of it. They prayed to Artemis (Diana) to bless their women, flocks and their fields.

The Ephesians also received praise for hating the practices of a group of divisive people called the *Nicolaitans.* The word *laitans* or *laity* means "people." The word *nico* means *to divide.* Apparently, the Nicolaitans were a divisive group of people who tried to splinter the church into groups and cliques.

However, in the midst of all these good deeds, the Ephesian Christians had "forsaken" their first love (2:4). They were very busy with Christian activities, but the thrill was gone.

Are you too busy working for God to walk with God? That's where the Ephesians were—their Christian walk had become a routine, instead of a relationship. To remedy this, Jesus instructs them to remember how it was when they first knew him and loved him. He wanted them to recall the hours in prayer they spent just talking with him and worshipping him.

Then he issued a warning—if they don't repent, he will "remove their lampstand (their influence) from its place" (2:5). What do you do with a burned-out light bulb? You set it aside—it's no longer useful. That's what Jesus is saying could happen to them. However, their reward for obeying is their right to eat from the Tree of Life (2:7). God allowed Adam and Eve to eat from it all they wanted. It was the Tree of the Knowledge of Good and Evil that was prohibited. When he banished them from the Garden of Eden, he placed cherubim to guard the Tree of Life so no one could eat from it.

What did this tree look like? If you are a Christian, you will see it for yourself one day in a prominent place in heaven, according to the end of Revelation.

Church in Smyrna

Beginning at Ephesus and ending with Laodicea, these seven churches make a geographic circle on an ancient map. Scholars believe the seven letters were sent to these churches even before John finished the rest of the Revelation. Jesus went from church to church, delivering a specific message that followed a specific pattern. This next church breaks the pattern, and it is one of the shortest letters. Jesus basically has only good things to say about this church. They are faithful, despite their affliction and poverty (2:9).

This congregation was poor because of persecution. In order to work, the members had to belong to a labor guild, almost like today's labor unions. However, every profession had a pagan deity. Guild members had to burn incense and bow before it. Christians who refused to do so lost their jobs and were poverty stricken.

Tertullian of Carthage was the pastor of a church in northern Africa around the year 200A.D., and some of the members of his congregation argued with him about this point. They rationalized the decision and said, "We must burn incense to this pagan god, even though we are Christians. We won't mean it, but we will do it." Tertullian said, "Why?" They said, "Because we have to work!" Tertullian said, "Why do you have to work?" They said, "Because we have to eat." He said, "Why do you have to eat?" They said, "Because we have to live." Tertullian then said, "No you don't have to work; you don't have to eat; and you don't have to live. The only thing you have to do is be faithful to God." The Smyrna Christians may have been poor financially, but Jesus said they were spiritually "rich" (2:9).

The early Church fathers write that the pastor of the church in Smyrna was named Polycarp. He was eventually arrested by the Romans and commanded to declare in a public place, "Caesar is Lord." Polycarp responded, "Eighty and six years have I served him [Jesus] and he never did me harm. How then can I blaspheme my King and my Savior?"

The Roman Proconsul said, "If you will not confess Caesar as Lord, I will burn you in the fire."

Polycarp replied, "You threaten me with fire, which burns for an hour and after a little is extinguished, but you are ignorant of the fire of the coming judgment and of eternal punishment reserved for the ungodly. Why are you waiting? Bring forth what you will." They tied him to a stake and the Jews in Smyrna gathered the wood for the fire. (This might have been why Jesus talks about those Jews who are of the synagogue of Satan in 2:9.) As he was dying, Polycarp prayed, "I thank thee that thou hast graciously thought me worthy of this day and of this hour that I may receive a portion in the number of thy martyrs in the cup of thy Christ." And he died.

Their promise for overcoming persecution is two-fold. In

2:10, they are given the crown of life. The Greek word here is *stephanos*, which describes the garland crown placed on the heads of athletes after winning a race. (And, by the way, we won't wear these crowns very long because we'll lay them at the feet of Jesus in heaven.) Jesus also rewards them in 2:11 by saying, "He who overcomes will not be hurt at all by the second death." The first death is physical death. That's inevitable. The second death is eternal separation from God, spiritual death.

When I travel, people ask me where I'm from because of my Southern accent. But what if somebody asked you, "Where are you from?" and you had to say, "Oh, I live where Satan lives." Jesus identifies the hometown of the next church as the very place where Satan had his throne.

Church in Pergamum

Pergamum was a place of great learning. In the ancient world, there were two cities with great libraries. First and most significant was the great library at Alexandria in northern Egypt with over 300,000 volumes. Tragically, when the Muslims overran Alexandria, they burned every scroll! The second greatest library in the ancient world was in Pergamum.

It was also known as a religious center. Many scholars believe Pergamum was the center of a Babylonian mystery cult described in detail in Revelation 17-18. Asclepius, the god of healing, was prominent in this city, and idol worship was prevalent. The symbol of Asclepius was a snake coiled around a staff, which is used today as a modern symbol of medicine. Despite this pagan setting, Jesus points out their faithfulness and commends them for not giving in to the secular culture surrounding them.

However, he chides them for allowing so-called religious people to unduly influence them. He references the story of Balak and Balaam in the Old Testament (Numbers 22-24). Balaam was a greedy prophet who unsuccessfully tried to have one foot in the world and one foot in God's Word, the temptation of all those living in worldly Pergamum.

They were also plagued by the Nicolaitans, the same problem those in Ephesus had successfully overcome. Another meaning of *nicolaitans* is to "rule over" the people, a problem that developed in the early Church in Rome and was not addressed until the Reformation in the 16th century. This problem still hasn't been corrected in many churches today. An artificial division developed between the clergy and the people. The clergy had special authority that other people didn't have. Jesus told the Ephesians early on that he "hated" this kind of distinction.

To encourage their obedience, he says, "To him who overcomes, I will give some of the hidden manna" (2:17). When the children of Israel left Egypt, God miraculously showered them with manna each morning. I've always thought of it as "sanctified Frosted Flakes," because the Bible describes it as small, round, flakes that were sweet to the taste.

To the Israelites who ate it every day, manna was a reminder of God's presence and provision. Jesus says to Pergamum, "If you'll be faithful, I promise I will give you all the manna (my presence) you need."

Jesus also promises the church in Pergamum another mysterious reward—a white stone with their name on it (2:17). In biblical times, two friends who were like family exchanged two halves of a flat white stone on which were written their nicknames. One could take that stone to the other's home, and their families would be bound to welcome them in. Jesus promises to do that for us. He wants to have such an intimate relationship with you that no one else on earth will have one exactly like it. And one day, he will welcome you home in heaven.

Church in Thyatira

This church was torn between two lovers. They loved Jesus, but they also loved someone in the church who was teaching heresy. Thyatira was known as a center for the garment industry, especially purple cloth. Lydia, who became a Christian in the book of Acts, was from the city of Thyatira, and she was known as a seller of purple garments. Of all seven churches, Thyatira is the most obscure.

Ironically, this church was the exact opposite of the church in Ephesus: they were more in love with Jesus now than they were at the first. Ephesus lost their first love, but Thyatira had grown stronger in their faith (2:19).

Still, Jesus has some strong words to this church regarding one woman, "Jezebel." Biblical scholars do not believe her name was literally Jezebel. (People seldom named their daughters Jezebel because of the terrible reputation Jezebel had in the Old Testament.) Jezebel married an Israelite king named Ahab and became a missionary for the worship of Baal, a sexually perverse cult. In Thyatira, this "Jezebel" was likewise leading church members to engage in sexual promiscuity, and Jesus called her on it. He gave her time to repent, but she was unwilling. He warned the church members of his coming judgment on her, and he encouraged all those who had not fallen prey to her teaching to stand firm and receive their reward.

CHAPTER 3

Special Delivery for the Churches

Church in Sardis

The North Star is some 30 light years away. If the star died, it would take the last bit of light 30 years to reach our eyes here on earth. It would be 30 years before we would even know that star *was dead*. The same can be said of some churches: they're dead; they just don't know it yet. In Revelation 3, Jesus addresses his comments to a dead church in Sardis. Sardis Christians were probably busy doing good works and meeting for church on a regular basis. In contrast, sometimes churches really don't want to accomplish much.

As a pastor, I attend annual associational meetings where representatives give reports on their churches. I actually heard a man from Alabama report on his church this way: "We didn't baptize nobody this year. We didn't have many new members, and we didn't take in very much money. We're not doing much at our church." Then he said, "But praise the Lord, none of the other churches around us are doing anything either." Sometimes churches think everything's great just because they are holding services!

W.A. Criswell once wrote about the difference between a live church and a dead church. He said, "Live churches are filled with folks with Bibles in their hands. Dead churches are not. Live churches have noisy children and youth. Dead churches do not. Live churches move by faith. Dead churches do not. Live churches have parking problems. Dead churches do not. Live churches emphasize opportunities, but dead churches focus on problems. Live churches are characterized by a loving fellowship. Dead churches manifest a bickering spirit. Live churches major on strong preaching. Dead churches emphasize liturgy. Live churches evangelize and dead churches fossilize."

I heard about a church that started with a lot of evangelistic zeal. They built a big sign outside the church that proclaimed, "JESUS Only." They lovingly shared Christ with their neighbors as the "only way of salvation." Through the years, the church began to deteriorate and decline in numbers. They allowed some ivy to grow over the sign until the letters "JES" were completely covered up. Instead of saying, "JESUS Only," the sign now read, "US Only." That's how churches die: being so inward-focused and caring only about themselves. Jesus stirred the Sardis believers from their spiritual slumber with two words: "Wake up!" (3:2). In fact, Jesus warned that if they kept hitting the "snooze button" on their spiritual alarm clock, it would be too late (3:3). This is not a time for you to be spiritually sleeping. Too much is at stake. Jesus Christ is going to rapture the Church—it could happen at anytime.

As a reward, Jesus says, "He who overcomes...will be dressed in white. I will never blot out his name from the book of life. I will acknowledge his name before my Father" (3:5). As we'll learn later on in Revelation, there is a Book of Life in heaven, and everyone whose name is in there will be saved.

Church in Philadelphia

Philadelphia comes from two Greek words: *philos* for "love" and *adelphos* for "brothers." Philadelphia literally means "the place where the brothers love one another; a place of brotherly love." This was not a city in the northeast of America. It was a very small, insignificant community in Asia Minor that made a big impression on the Lord Jesus. This church has often been called, "The Church of the Open Door" because Jesus says, "I have placed before you an open door that no one can shut" (3:8). Life is full of doors—think of them as opportunities to be seized through the choices you make. Satan often tries to shut the door if going through it will bring you closer to Christ. However, Jesus said in Luke 11:9, "Knock [and keep on knocking] and the door will be opened to you."

Jesus praised them for holding on with the "little strength" that they had (3:8). There are some Christians who have so much money, so much intelligence and so much natural ability they don't feel as if they need God's strength. They have everything handled. However, Paul wrote that when you know you are weak, God makes you that much stronger (2 Corinthians 12:9-10). As a reward for their faithfulness, Jesus promised them divine protection from those in the "synagogue of Satan" (3:9-10). There were some people, even in this good church, who were professing to be children of God—yet they were anything but.

Second, Jesus promises protection from "the hour of trial" (3:10), a reference to the end times. This is another key verse regarding the promise that Jesus will rapture the Church before the Tribulation begins. He promises protection from the "hour of trial" or "tribulation," which is the word *thlipsis*.

He says this Tribulation "is going to come upon the whole world to test those who live on the earth." In Matthew 24:21, Jesus describes the "great distress, unequaled from the beginning of the world until now—and never to be equaled again." This is the trial from which we will be protected, and it's a strong promise that the Church won't be around during this time of tribulation.

Church in Laodicea

If you could stick a spiritual thermometer into your heart, what would it read? Cold? Hot? Somewhere in between? A lukewarm Christian is *neutral* spiritually. They don't get upset about much of anything, and they refuse to take a stand on moral issues. It's like a politician being asked about a pressing issue who says, "Some of my friends are for it. Some of my friends are against it. I agree with my friends."

Vance Havner said, "In the twentieth century, most of us have become so subnormal in our Christian life that when someone comes along and begins to act normal, we label them as abnormal." Many Christians have collectively cooled off our Christianity to the point that we're uncomfortable being around a "normal New Testament Christian" because they want to talk about Jesus all the time! Jesus described the Laodicean congregation as lukewarm—like coffee that has been sitting out too long—and it literally made him sick (3:16).

Laodicea was the wealthiest congregation of these seven churches in a center of financial affairs and medical practice. On a typical Sunday at Laodicea, you would have seen folks with Rolex sundials on their wrists and the finest chariots parked outside—some with two-horse power and some with four-horse power. They had everything they needed in terms of wealth and possessions. But their wealth prevented them from being totally dependent on the Lord.

In this chapter, Jesus tells us very clearly what to do when we find ourselves in a spiritually lukewarm condition. First, he told them to change their value system (3:18). People are living under one of two kingdoms. Some are living under the "thingdom" of gold. Others are living under the "kingdom" of God. Gold was the standard in Laodicea, but Jesus counseled them to exchange their fool's gold for what was truly valuable. In the city known for its garment industry, Jesus counseled them to exchange their linen for his "white clothes" of purity. In a city that was making mega-bucks for selling eye salve, Jesus wanted to open their eyes so they could really see what was going on and shake their complacency.

The Vision Begins

Maybe there was a time when your life was characterized by a greater zeal for Jesus Christ. However, through the years your faith may have become cold and dark like abandoned coals around a campfire. If there is one thing a study of Revelation can and should do, it is to reignite your desire to know and serve Christ.

The next chapter in the book of Revelation marks the start of some sobering descriptions of the future. And that time is closer now than it's ever been.

CHAPTER 4

Throne Room of Heaven

In *The Lion, the Witch and the Wardrobe*, by C.S. Lewis, an old wardrobe becomes the magical doorway to another land. Lucy, the main character, steps through the wardrobe and into a snowy forest scene where she encounters creatures and characters from this other world. When she returns back home, she tries describing what she's seen, but it's difficult for the others to understand the wonder of all she has experienced. In Revelation chapter 4, Jesus beckons John toward an open door in heaven. This marks the beginning of a series of unusual visions and encounters John has that can only be described as something from another world. This also marks the beginning of our third and final section in our Table of Contents from 1:19. This is the future—what Jesus says "will take place later."

The World of Heaven

Seldom has the veil of heaven been drawn back enabling us to see what is there. Daniel described a brief look at God. Moses got a glimpse of the afterglow of God on Mt. Sinai. As Stephen was being stoned to death, he looked up and said he saw heaven open and Jesus standing at God's right hand. However, in John's vision, we see the clearest picture of what heaven is like.

Some picture heaven as a beautiful golf course where you never slice the ball and all your putts roll in. Some think of heaven as a place where we float on fluffy clouds like angels, playing a harp and eating Milky Way candy bars for all eternity. Others think heaven is going to be a serene place of exquisite beauty. However, what's going to catch your attention in heaven is not "some-thing"; it's someone. The single thing that will make heaven "heaven" is the fact that Jesus will be there. Even if there weren't streets of gold, gates of pearl and a crystal sea, heaven would be heaven enough for me if only Jesus were there.

The Rapture of the Church

The opening lines of 4:1-2 describe an interlude between what Jesus said to the churches and the beginning of John's vision of the future. But it's a very important two-verse interlude because it references the time when the Church will be taken out before the Tribulation begins.

Although the word "rapture" doesn't appear in English in the Bible, it is the Greek word *harpazo* found in 1 Thessalonians 4:17 which describes Christians being "caught up" with Jesus in the air. The Latin Vulgate translation of the Bible uses the word *rapio*, where we get our word *rapture*. We call this event the "Rapture of the Church."

In fact, when you read Revelation 4:1 and Paul's description of the Rapture in 1 Thessalonians 4:16-17 side-by-side, you see unmistakable similarities. First, there is a "shout" or "loud command" like a trumpet that signals Christ's appearing. Paul described it and John actually heard it. First Thessalonians 4:16-17 says:

> For the Lord himself will come down from heaven, *with a loud command,* with the voice of the archangel and *with the trumpet call* of God, and the

> dead in Christ will rise first. After that, we who are still alive and are left will be caught up together with them in the clouds to meet the Lord in the air. And so we will be with the Lord forever.

John heard Jesus say, "Come up here" to heaven with him (4:1). Then, John was "at once" caught up into heaven. What happens to the Church at the Rapture occurs with the same sense of immediacy. Paul says we will be "immediately" caught up in heaven, and 1 Corinthians 15:52 describes it as happening so fast it's like a flash or the twinkling of an eye. Blinking and twinkling are not the same things, by the way. See how fast you can blink your eye right now. The Rapture is faster than that. The human eye blinks about one four hundredth of a second. The twinkling of an eye is the time it takes your brain to see someone you are looking for and recognize them–that's the twinkling of an eye. Some people think when Jesus comes to rapture the Church, they are going to have time to get on their knees and repent—as if he's gently floating down with a parachute. No, it will occur suddenly—as suddenly as John found himself transported from the beach at Patmos to heaven.

When Will This Happen?

There are varying interpretations on the timing of the Rapture, as it relates to the Tribulation. Some Christians believe they are going to live through the entire Tribulation. Some Christians believe they will be "caught up" with Jesus in heaven at some point halfway during the Tribulation. Based on my studies of Scripture and the research of many other conservative pastors and theologians who feel the same way, I firmly believe the Church has been transported into heaven at the beginning of Revelation 4. We will not take part in any of the Tribulation.

So, what does John see once he meets up with Jesus in heaven? What he describes next is a throne room unlike any earthly one you've ever seen.

Fit for a King

One summer on our return from a mission trip in Russia, our group stopped at the Kremlin in Moscow and toured the armory of Catherine the Great and the Russian czars. We saw several Fabergé eggs—intricate, jeweled eggs worth several million dollars each. Then we entered a room displaying the ornate gold thrones from the former czars. One throne made of pure gold was twice as wide and twice as high as a modern recliner. Every square inch was embedded with precious stones. Those thrones are priceless. But the world has yet to see the greatest throne since the beginning of creation, and that is the throne of God in heaven.

There are seven lamps blazing before the throne—representing the perfection (remember "seven") of the Holy Spirit (4:5). It's not just what John sees that is so amazing; it's what he hears as peals of thunder and flashes of lightning emanate from this majestic throne. John also describes a rainbow that encircles it (4:3). From our perspective here on the ground, we can only see half of a rainbow. However, every pilot knows that rainbows are actually complete circles.

There is Someone seated on the throne, and that's where John's focus is directed. At this point, John doesn't know who he is, but those around the throne give us some clues that the One seated on the throne is very important.

Who Sits around the Throne?

Some say the 24 elders around God's throne in 4:4 are angels, but these elders have been redeemed and where white robes of righteousness, the righteousness of Christ. And since angels have never been lost, they have no need to be redeemed. Also, innumerable angels are mentioned as a different group encircling the throne (5:11) giving praise to Jesus. So, these are not angels.

Other interpretations of the 24 elders say they are the twelve patriarchs from the Old Testament and the twelve Apostles from the New Testament. However, most conservative scholars believe these 24 elders represent all the redeemed, of all the ages. Twelve represent all the Old Testament redeemed saints who were saved under the Old Covenant. Old Testament believers like Moses, Isaiah and Elijah had faith in God's plan, and God's plan was Jesus. They just didn't know his name. The other twelve represent "us" (all the New Testament saints redeemed under the New Covenant). If you don't realize what these elders represent, much of the rest of Revelation is going to unravel for you, and you will be confused.

Unique Heavenly Attendants

The four living creatures are before the throne. One has the face of a lion; one has the face of an ox; one has the face of a man; and one has the face of an eagle. These four creatures are constantly encircling the throne, praising God from the foundation of creation. But why the four faces? I believe they reflect the One they see—Jesus. Have you ever wondered why we have four different gospel accounts in Matthew, Mark, Luke and John? Why don't we just have one? Each one tells a different perspective of the character of Jesus. If you were drawing a picture of me from the front, back, left side and right side, they would be four different pictures, but it would be the same person. Each writer, inspired by the Holy Spirit, emphasized a different angle of Jesus' character.

The four gospel accounts also parallel the faces on these four creatures. A lion is the king of the jungle, and Matthew primarily describes Jesus as the King. Mark often represents Jesus as a servant, which is symbolized by an ox, a beast of burden. Dr. Luke describes Jesus as the Son of man, and the third creature has the face of a man. John concentrates on the deity of Jesus, which is like the fourth creature: a soaring eagle pictured high above everything on earth. These creatures could simply be four reflections of Jesus himself.

John writes in 4:8 that the four living creatures constantly praise God: "Day and night they never stop saying, 'Holy, holy, holy.'" This is similar to the vision of God's throne in Isaiah 6 where Isaiah saw six seraphs (a special kind of angel) with four wings crying out the same words of praise. The four living creatures repeat the word "holy" three times: for the Father, the Son and the Holy Spirit. But why don't these creatures say, "Great, great, great" or "Wise, wise, wise" or "Love, love, love"? According to the Bible, *holy* is the best word to describe God's character—he is infinitely "other" than anything or anyone else.

Note the reaction of the elders who are in the very

presence of God. They fall down on their faces in worship. If we want to be ready to meet the Lord, we need to be prepared to fall down at his feet (4:10). If the President of the United States walked in a room, everyone would stand to their feet as a sign of respect. However, when we see Jesus, we will not respectfully stand to our feet; we will fall to our faces.

Do you sometimes do that now in prayer? Are there times when you lie facedown before him in prayer and it seems you can't get your face deep enough in the carpet? That's the attitude of those who have been redeemed.

The point of this passage is to remind you that how you worship him *now* in your daily life is preparing you to worship him *then* for eternity. The love and adoration you have in your heart now is going to be multiplied when you get there! Sometimes we are slow to enter into an attitude of worship in church, and we just go through the motions. When you are truly worshiping God, you won't be concerned about what the person beside you thinks. You will be focused on God. I guarantee that when you get to heaven, you're not going to be thinking about what the other believer beside you is thinking about the way you sing.

The two short hymns of praise from the creatures and elders worshipping are called "doxologies" (4:8,11). Throughout Revelation, these doxologies build upon themselves in ever-increasing measure. In Revelation 1:6, there are only two descriptions ascribing "glory and honor" to God. Chapter 4:11 adds to that and says to give him "glory and honor and power." In 5:13, the song of praise becomes "glory and honor and power and majesty." Later in 7:12, it increases to "glory and honor and majesty and power and praise." These doxologies grow even greater as the prophecy unfolds. The more we read about heaven and the greatness of God, the more we want to praise him. Revelation is one of the greatest inspirations for increasing your understanding of and your desire to worship.

Who Is Worthy?

In Revelation 5, all of heaven is looking for someone worthy to open an important scroll. And there is only one who is able to do so. When he steps up to read it, the most incredible scene plays out before John's eyes.

CHAPTER 5

One is Worthy

A traditional book has binding on its spine, but bound books did not exist until about the third century after Jesus. As a precursor to bound books, early believers took Old Testament scrolls and tied them together on the ends, securing each section with a seal. The scroll John describes has seven seals. We don't know exactly what those seals looked like, but whoever opened the scroll and broke the first seal unwound the first section and so on until the whole scroll and all the seals were opened.

In 5:1-2, John says, "Then I saw in the right hand of him who sat on the throne a scroll with writing on both sides and sealed with seven seals. And I saw a mighty angel proclaiming in a loud voice, 'Who is worthy to break the seals and open the scroll?'"

What Could Have Been Ours

What does this scroll symbolize? Scrolls were often used to record deeds and official details about inheritances. Think of this scroll as representing our forfeited inheritance—which is all that God originally intended for Adam and Eve to experience in the Garden of Eden. However, sin caused us to forfeit that inheritance. Let me put this in the language of Hebrew real estate. In the Old Testament, when someone was at risk of losing his or her property, only a legal kinsman (called a *go'el*, literally "a redeemer/kinsman") could buy it back. In other words, only another member of the family could pay the price and redeem the property deed that was always contained in some kind of a sealed document like the one we see in Revelation.

The book of Ruth illustrates this principle through the story of a widow named Naomi who moves back to Bethlehem after being away and wants to reclaim her property. However, she cannot buy it back herself—she needs a kinsman redeemer to do it for her. Boaz claimed his right as the legal kinsman (and marries Naomi's daughter-in-law, Ruth, in the process!). There was another qualified kinsman who chose not to be the kinsman-redeemer. But Boaz was both willing and able to fulfill that role. When he paid the price, he was given the scroll of the deed for the property. He was the only one "worthy" to do so.

That's what's happening in Revelation 5. The angel is seeking a kinsman-redeemer who is both willing and able to redeem what humanity forfeited at the Fall. Jesus is the only one who can do that for us. "Redeem" means "to buy back." We have already been *redeemed* by the price paid on Calvary, but Jesus has not yet *reclaimed* our lost inheritance as described here. When the Bible speaks of the end times, it says: "When these things begin to take place, stand up and lift up your heads, because your redemption is drawing near" (Luke 21:28). That's future tense. In a sense, our redemption has not been *completed* until Jesus takes this scroll with seven seals, the title deed to what God intended for humanity—our redemption.

A "Slain" Lamb

Of course, John doesn't understand all this as he sees this scene unfold in heaven. He actually weeps because the angel says no one is qualified to take the scroll or even to see what's inside. Mohammed can't take the scroll. Confucius can't take the scroll. Buddha can't take the scroll. But then one of the elders says to John, "Do not weep! See, the Lion of the tribe of Judah, the Root of David, has triumphed. He is able to open the scroll and its seven seals" (5:5).

John looks up with teary eyes and he sees a Lamb, "looking as if it had been slain." On the day of Yom Kippur, the Day of Atonement, the high priest took a curved, sharp blade and slit the throat of a sacrificial lamb, pouring its blood on the altar. However, this slain Lamb in Revelation is still standing. You would expect a slain sacrifice to fall down. Jesus, who was slain from the foundation of the world at the cross, is alive and well!

The Bible says this Lamb "had seven horns and seven eyes which are the seven spirits of God sent out into all the earth" (5:6). Don't be afraid of the beautiful symbolism in the book of Revelation. Trying to visualize Jesus, the Lamb of God, with seven horns and seven eyes will make you feel like you've having some sort of nightmare! Remember, this is all symbolic. The number "seven" once more signifies perfection.

And the Crowd Goes Wild

As Jesus assumes the scroll, the four living creatures and the 24 elders fall down before him once more in worship. Then the angels join in to praise him. John uses a word for the number of angels that literally translates in Greek as *innumerable.* It is the Greek word, *murias*, where we get our word *myriads*—meaning tens of thousands. One morning in 1938, a physicist was looking out on his lawn and contemplating the innumerable dewdrops out it. He said to his nine-year-old son, "How many dewdrops do you think there are out there in our yard?" His son looked out and said, "There must be googols." That's where the number "googol" originated. It is a 1 with a hundred zeroes.

Can you imagine googol squared? Googol to the hundredth power? It's a number so large we can't comprehend it.

In verse 9, where the elders are worshipping, the word used is literally "sing." We are singing a new song before the Lord. The New International Version (NIV) translation also uses the word "sang" in 5:12 to describe how the angels worship God. However, in the Greek, it is the word *lego*—which means they "spoke" or shouted their praise. Imagine hundreds of thousands of angels shouting their praise! "Worthy is the Lamb, who was slain, to receive power and wealth and wisdom and strength and honor and glory and praise!" (5:12).

There is one final pinnacle of praise beginning in verse 13: "Then I heard every creature in heaven and on earth and under the earth and on the sea and all that is in them, singing…" Again, it is the word *lego,* so we are all *shouting* "to him who sits on the throne and to the Lamb be praise and honor and glory and power for ever and ever!'" Even the most powerful worship services we've ever been a part of here on earth are *nothing* compared to what it's going to be like when we get into heaven!

If you've ever tried imagining what heaven will be like,

John gives us a wonderful glimpse of what will take place. But what about those who are not Christians when Jesus comes back to rapture the Church? What will happen to them?

We will take a look at that in the next chapter because as the seals start being opened and God's judgment starts pouring out on the earth, it signals the beginning of seven years of the Tribulation. Why seven years? The answer is found in Daniel 9. He prophesied there would be 70 weeks in which God would complete everything in his plan. The Hebrew word means "seven" and in this context means seven years, not seven days. The first 69 "weeks" (483 years) was the time between Daniel's prophecy and when the Messiah was crucified. God's prophetic clock stopped then. We're living right now between the 69th and 70th "weeks" on God's prophetic calendar. The 70th "week" is the seven-year Tribulation, which starts to unfold in chapter 6.

CHAPTER 6

Judgment Begins

Beginning in chapter 6, the scene shifts from heaven to planet earth to describe what is taking place while believers are in heaven. And it's not a pretty picture. The good news is if you are a Christian, you are not going to be here on earth when all of this is taking place. One reason you *don't* want to take your time waiting to accept Jesus as your Savior is that you won't want to be left behind to experience this terrible world chaos. There is nothing more that has to happen on God's prophetic calendar for the rapture of the Church to take place and the seven-year Tribulation to begin. It could happen at any time.

In Revelation chapters 6-18, we're going to look at three series of sevens that describe God's judgment on the earth. There are seven seals, then seven trumpets and then seven bowls of wrath poured on the earth. These three series of sevens (seals, trumpets and bowls) all have the same sequence. The first four are described quickly, and then there is a pause before the numbers five and six are given. Then there is a longer pause, after which the seventh is given. Each one of these seals, trumpets and bowls reveal a judgment more terrible than the last.

In Matthew 24, Jesus describes every one of these same judgments in the same order they are listed in Revelation 6. The same thing John described as taking place in the Tribulation is the same thing that Jesus predicted would happen. Let's go through each seal and see what's in store for those who remain on the earth after the Rapture.

Seal #1: Deceptive Peacemaker

> I watched as the Lamb opened the first of seven seals. Then, I heard one of the four living creatures say in a voice like thunder, "Come!" I looked and there before me was a white horse! Its rider held a bow, and he was given a crown, and he rode out as a conqueror bent on conquest. (Revelation 6:1-2)

The opening of the first four seals summons four horsemen who represent frightening scenarios unfolding on earth during the Tribulation. The first horse's rider appears to be someone rather benign in his intentions. He is symbolically riding a white horse, and we all know good guys wear white hats and ride the white horses, right? In fact, we're going to see when Jesus returns in chapter 19 that Jesus is going to be riding a white horse also. But this first rider represents Satan's *imitation* of Jesus: the counterfeit Christ, the Antichrist who becomes a world-recognized leader.

The Antichrist's horse is white, meaning bloodless. This rider is somehow able to take control of the world in a bloodless coup, slipping in as a peaceful ruler. In ancient military days, when a general was surrendering, he would ride up to the opposing army holding up a bow with no arrow, like this rider. The Antichrist comes on the scene when Jesus has raptured the Church and millions have inexplicably disappeared from earth, spawning a crisis the world has never known! This magnanimous ruler steps up and proposes that all the bewildered nations work together now to solve the world's problems. No more nationalism. No more pitting

country against country. Doesn't that sound attractive? It will be when the world is in a state of mass confusion right after the Rapture.

Seal #2: Military Chaos

> When the Lamb opened the second seal, I heard the second living creature say, "Come!" Then another horse came out, a fiery red one. Its rider was given power to take peace from the earth and to make men slay each other. To him was given a large sword. (Revelation 6:3)

This other horse and rider represent the onslaught of widespread warfare on the earth. In World War I, 10 million people died. In World War II, 50 million people died. However, this scene is predicting a time in the future when the entire world will be entangled in global warfare, and many more people are going to die. The great sword this rider carries is the Greek word *machaira,* which means a dagger. In Bible times, the zealots carried a dagger in the sleeves of their robes and used it in guerrilla-style warfare or what we call terrorism. It could be this is a prediction of the widespread prevalence of terrorism as a major policy of the Antichrist.

Seal #3: Deadly Poverty

> When the Lamb opened the third seal, I heard the third living creature say, "Come!" I looked and there before me was a black horse! Its rider was holding a pair of scales in his hand. Then I heard what sounded like a voice among the four living creatures, saying, "A quart of wheat for a day's wages, and three quarts of barley for a day's wages, and do not damage the oil and the wine!" (Revelation 6:5-6)

The first seal deals with political judgment through the rule of the Antichrist. The second seal addresses military judgment. This third seal has to do with economic judgment and worldwide poverty. There will be so much war going on at this time that people don't have time to plant their crops. When a nation can't produce food, the result is famine and poverty. The Bible says one quart of wheat will equal a day's wages. In John's day during good economic times, one man working all day made enough money to feed himself, his family and to pay for his living expenses. However, one quart of wheat is only enough to feed one person. Times are going to be so bad economically that a man works all day, and he only makes enough food to feed his own mouth, not his wife nor his children. It's going to be a devastating time of economic collapse.

The reference to "oil and wine" is like our "caviar and champagne" today—luxury items for the rich and famous. Some people are going to be living in luxury while much of the world is living in poverty. We see that already happening today. The middle class is shrinking, and our world is segregating into two classes: the very rich and the very poor.

Seal #4: Earthly Pandemics

> When the Lamb opened the fourth seal, I heard the voice of the fourth living creature say, "Come!" I looked, and there before me was a pale horse! Its rider was named Death, and Hades was following close behind him. They were given power over a fourth of the earth to kill by sword, famine and plague, and by the wild beasts of the earth. (Revelation 6:7-8)

Warfare leads to famine, which leads to pestilence, which leads to Death—the name of this pale horse's rider. During

World War I, almost 20 million died of influenza. Another 6.5 million died from other diseases. This fourth seal is describing a time in the future where disease is going to be rampant worldwide.

We've already seen the spread of anti-viral resistant diseases like H1N1 and other near-pandemics in our world. This is the very kind of widespread pestilence the Bible describes. Some experts warn that the continued urbanization of population centers around the world could lead to an increase in vermin and rats. That's how the Bubonic Plague spread through Europe and killed 25% of the population in the 14th Century. Could rats be the "wild beasts" this passage is talking about in verse 8? We don't have to know the details; it's enough to know there will be unsurpassed pestilence.

Seal #5: Global Persecution

> When he opened the fifth seal, I saw under the altar the souls of those who had been slain because of the word of God and the testimony they had maintained. They called out in a loud voice, "How long, Sovereign Lord, holy and true, until you judge the inhabitants of the earth and avenge our blood?" Then each of them was given a white robe, and they were told to wait a little longer, until the number of their fellow servants and brothers who were to be killed as they had been was completed. (Revelation 6:9-11)

This passage is obviously referring to martyrs, although not the Christians who have been martyred through the centuries. Remember, the Church has been raptured and the dead in Christ have been raised at this time. This passage is talking about a unique group of people we are going to see many more times in the book of Revelation called

Tribulation saints. They are saved during the Tribulation, and many of them will die as martyrs. Today, extreme religious persecution is isolated to certain parts of the world where it is actually illegal to be a Christian. We're blessed that we don't yet have to experience that in the United States. In the Tribulation, people of every nation will be persecuted unto death for their faith in Jesus Christ.

Seal #6: Widespread Panic

> I watched as he opened the sixth seal. There was a great earthquake. The sun turned black like sackcloth made of goat hair, the whole moon turned blood red, and the stars in the sky fell to earth, as late figs drop from a fig tree when shaken by a strong wind. The sky receded like a scroll, rolling up, and every mountain and island was removed from its place. (Revelation 6:12-14)

Have you seen pictures of the tests of the first atomic bomb exploded by the United States before Hiroshima and Nagasaki? It seems as if the sky "rolled up like a scroll" in a mushroom-shaped cloud. One can imagine a nuclear explosion on a grand scale would turn the sky red and cause an eclipse. The reaction of the people on earth would be absolute panic! The conclusion of chapter 6 describes everyone hiding and living in the rocks for safety. This event will be so terrifying that people will long to kill themselves to escape it, but they won't be able to do so.

A Pause in Heaven

Between the sixth and the seventh seal, the sixth and the seventh trumpet and the sixth and the seventh bowl there is a pause. That may be a little confusing in the chronology if you don't understand God is simply putting a "parenthesis" between the sixth seal and the seventh seal. I call this pause "The Eye of the Storm," because after six seals were opened and the terrible judgment, there's a period of relative calm and rest. We finally get a glimpse of some good news in the midst of this chaos as we meet a special group of people set aside for God's purpose.

CHAPTER 7

God's People Set Apart

In chapter 7, God puts a seal on the foreheads of 144,000 of the Jews and protects them from the coming wrath. This word "seal" is the same idea mentioned in Ephesians 1:13 where God seals believers with the Holy Spirit. It literally means, "to be protected, guarded."

As I've said, Israel plays a prominent role in the end times. Throughout the Old Testament, we read about ancient people groups like the Jebusites, the Edomites and the Moabites—but where are they today? They are no longer on this earth. But can you find an Israelite today? Sure, you can! For centuries, the Jews have maintained their unique identity, when other ancient peoples of the earth have not.

God has been preserving Israel for a purpose. Paul explains in Romans 11:25, "I do not want you to be ignorant of this mystery, brothers, so that you may not be conceited. Israel has experienced a hardening in part *until the full number of the Gentiles has come in.*" Right now, the Jews persist in unbelief because they do not accept Jesus as the Messiah. However, after the full number of the Gentiles (non-Jews) has come into the kingdom (accepted Christ) and the Church is raptured, Israel is going to become God's prime directive again. In the future Tribulation, these 144,000 Jews are going to go around the world preaching the Gospel. We know what one Jewish evangelist could do—the Apostle Paul. Imagine what would happen if we multiplied his zeal times 144,000! We'll learn more about this special group in Revelation 14.

The second half of chapter 7 is devoted to another special group of people in the Tribulation. They are called the Tribulation saints.

The Tribulation Saints

I heard a funny story about a man who was a moonshiner, a drug runner, a terrible husband and father and a gambler who never set foot in church. He was very wealthy because of his illicit activities. When he died, the pastor of the local church was asked to do the funeral. The dead man's brother, John, said to the pastor, "Everybody knows what a terrible man my brother was. But, Pastor, I want you to stand up at the funeral service and say he was a saint." The pastor refused. His brother expected that, so then he offered him $100,000 towards the church's building program "if you will just say my brother was a saint." The leery pastor sighed and said, "I'll think about it."

The next day, the church was packed, wanting to know what the poor pastor would say about this troublemaker. The pastor stood behind the casket, took a deep breath and said, "You all knew this man. You know he was a reprobate and an infidel who never darkened the doors of this church. He was a moonshiner and a drug runner. And not only that, he was a terrible husband and a terrible father. But compared to his brother, John, he was a saint!"

When you hear the word *saint*, what do you think of? Some may think of the New Orleans Saints or a St. Christopher medal. Actually, a saint is simply someone who has been redeemed. The Tribulation saints are those who will be saved during the Tribulation. Some claim that during the Tribulation no one will be saved. However, that's not the case. Many will be saved, and we read about them in the second half of Revelation 7. They are the Tribulation saints because one of the elders identifies this group as having "come out of the great tribulation" (7:14).

> After this I looked and there before me was a great multitude that no one could count, from every nation, tribe, people and language, standing before the throne and in front of the Lamb. They were wearing white robes and were holding palm branches in their hands. Then one of the elders asked me, "These in white robes—who are they, and where did they come from?" I answered, "Sir, you know." And he said, "These are they who have come out of the great tribulation; they have washed their robes and made them white in the blood of the Lamb." (Revelation 7:9, 13-14)

I want to make a distinction between them and what we call New Testament believers, the Church. Because I hold to what's called a "pre-tribulation" belief in eschatology (the study of end times) I believe the Church is raptured out before the Tribulation begins. They are represented by the 24 elders, who are also part of this passage. The description of the people who are saved *during* the time of tribulation who are martyred because of their belief in Jesus Christ is a different group—the Tribulation saints.

Some Christians who believe in a mid-tribulation Rapture (where the Church is raptured midway through the Tribulation) point to this passage as evidence to support their belief. They say this passage is describing Christians today undergoing the future Tribulation and leaving midway through it. To prove that these are two different groups, let's compare the 24 elders (the Church) with the Tribulation saints.

Dressing

In chapters 4 and 5, the elders are wearing white garments. The Tribulation saints in 7:13 are wearing white "robes" according to the NIV translation. However, the word used there is actually the Greek word *stole,* which is not a garment per se. It's where we get our word for "stole," something wrapped around one's shoulders.

Placement

We've already learned in an earlier chapter that the 24 elders are seated on thrones around the Lamb (4:4). This new group of Tribulation saints is described as "standing before the throne and in front of the Lamb" (7:9).

Crowns

If you recall from an earlier chapter, the Bible says we (the elders) are wearing crowns of gold on our heads (4:4), which we lay before the throne in worship. This group of Tribulation saints is not pictured as wearing crowns.

Harps

In earlier scenes, the elders are pictured playing harps (5:8). Look carefully: the Tribulation saints are holding palms instead.

Praising

The 24 elders are "singing a new song" (5:9). This passage doesn't say the Tribulation saints sing. Like the angels earlier, they too are "shouting" aloud their praise (7:10).

Position

The elders are pictured earlier ruling and reigning with Christ (5:10). However, this group of Tribulation saints is pictured as servants of God (7:15).

There are enough differences between these two groups that I don't think the Bible is talking about the same group. That's why I'm convinced the 24 elders represent us, and the Tribulation saints are a unique group of believers who express their faith during the terrible Tribulation.

Heaven Welcomes the Tribulation Saints

The Bible says these special saints who come out of the Tribulation will never experience hunger and thirst again. In Revelation 13, we'll learn that the Antichrist will require everyone to receive a special symbol (a "mark of the beast") on his or her head or hand in order to buy and sell food. These saints refuse to accept the sign, so they become social outcasts who will suffer outside under the heat of the sun.

But when they arrive in heaven, those dark days are over. To emphasize this truth, John employs a couple of Greek double negatives. A double negative is like saying, "Don't never use double negatives because it's bad grammar." In the Greek language, double negatives don't cancel each other out; they *intensify* the force of a statement. Chapter 7:16 literally says, "Never, no never, no never again will they hunger. Never, no never, no never again will they thirst. The sun will not never, no never beat upon them nor never, never any scorching heat." God gives them a powerful promise of provision in heaven. Not only are they protected, but also they will be refreshed by living water.

Have you ever heard someone say that there will be no tears in heaven? We know of at least one time when there are tears because God wipes them away from the eyes of these martyrs. These Tribulation saints will have suffered terrible persecution and torture at the hand of the wicked Antichrist. Many of their family members were killed before their eyes. They are weeping from exhaustion and the deep sorrow they experienced in the Tribulation, and like weary soldiers coming out of a war, they are crying. This is just one more reason why you *do not want to be left behind when Jesus raptures the Church!*

What will it be like the first Sunday after Jesus comes back? Like our nation one week after 9-11, I predict the church buildings are going to be packed. Some will realize they were counterfeit Christians who were never really saved. Tragically, they have now been left behind on earth to experience the tragedy of the Tribulation. It's possible that some of them will now accept Christ during the Tribulation, but they will pay a steep price with their lives.

The Eye of the Storm Passes

At the beginning of chapter 8, the eye of the storm has passed. The wrath of God resumes once more as the seventh seal is opened up, and it ushers in an event that has never before happened in heaven.

CHAPTER 8

Hurled on the Earth

Imagine a wondrous worship service with millions of people caught up in praise—then imagine it coming to a complete and sudden halt. As far as we know, this verse in Revelation 8:1 describes the only time there is silence in heaven. Otherwise, heaven is buzzing with activity amidst an everlasting praise song. The seventh seal is merely a transition leading into the next series of "seven," which are seven trumpets. As you might expect in this pattern, the seventh trumpet is then going to lead into the seven bowls of wrath, too. However, this moment of silence doesn't last long. Soon, the judgments are in full force again—and these are much worse. At this point in Revelation, it's the middle of the Tribulation, and the suffering accelerates.

Angels in Heaven

Chapter 8:2-5 says:

> And I saw the seven angels who stand before God, and to them were given seven trumpets. Another angel, who had a golden censer [an ornate, burning lamp hanging from a chain in which incense is burned] came and stood at the altar. He was given much incense to offer, with the prayers of all the saints, on the golden altar before the throne. The smoke of the incense, together with the prayers of the saints, went up before God from the angel's hand. Then the angel took the censer, filled it with fire from the altar, and hurled it on the earth; and there came peals of thunder, rumblings, flashes of lightning and an earthquake.

These seven "Trumpet Angels" announce the next series of judgments on the earth. In ancient warfare (and as late as the American mounted cavalry), trumpets played a very important role. In battle, a different trumpet tune would signal whether the troops should attack or retreat. Trumpets were used in communities to announce a public gathering such as the inauguration of a new leader. Now, these seven angels blow their trumpets to signal the arrival of judgment.

There is speculation that one of them is Gabriel. In Luke 1:19, Gabriel appears to Zechariah and says, "I am Gabriel. I stand in the presence of the Lord!" Popular songs refer to Gabriel blowing his horn in the end times, but his name is not used in specific connection with these trumpets in Scripture.

Priestly Angel

Along with the seven, there is another angel I'm going to call a "priestly angel" who carries a censer filled with incense (8:3). Some commentators believe this is the Lord Jesus Christ because he is our High Priest. I personally don't believe that because Jesus is never veiled in Revelation—he is clearly pictured as the Lamb on the throne.

I'll never forget the first time I visited Jerusalem. We went within the city walls to the Church of the Holy Sepulcher. I walked in and saw hundreds of gold censers hanging from the ceiling, all of them filled with burning incense. The pungent smoke was so thick that I could hardly breathe! For the Eastern Orthodox Church, burning incense is a very important part of worship. As this fragrant odor floats up into the air, it's a picture of prayers, adoration and worship going up toward God.

In our Revelation scene here, something else besides the incense is rising up before God; it is "the prayers of all the saints" (8:3). The prayers you pray now are heard in heaven, and they are stored up (like a back-up drive in your computer). The time is going to come in the future when, once again, your prayers will ascend before God as a pleasing fragrance. Some have suggested that these may be prayers of worship and adoration, rather than prayers of petition. Why is that? When you ask God a request, you are taking something *out of* heaven. But when you pray a prayer of praise, you are putting something *in heaven.*

Anguish on the Earth

Suddenly, the priestly angel shatters this peaceful moment and hurls the censer down to the earth. That's when the other seven angels pick up their trumpets and prepare to announce the coming judgment. Let's look at what each trumpet brings forth.

Trumpet #1 Ecological disaster: Nuclear holocaust?

> Then the seven angels who had the seven trumpets prepared to sound them. The first angel sounded his trumpet and there came hail and fire mixed with blood, and it was hurled down upon the earth. A third of the earth was burned up, a third of the trees were burned up, and all the green grass was burned up. (Revelation 8:6-7)

Activists often talk about how fragile our ecology is, warning us of a pending disastrous chain reaction that will destroy the plants and animals on the earth. The Bible says something on that grand scale is actually going to happen. Of course, some may ask at this point, "Is this literal or symbolic?" Let me give you a great tool to use in interpreting all Scripture, whether you're reading Genesis, Revelation, Ephesians or Nahum. You should always take the Bible literally at first glance, unless there is obvious symbolism employed (and you can always tell if there is). If there is obvious symbolism, then look for the literal truth of that symbol. But always take God's truth literally.

Therefore, I believe what this passage says is literal; it describes exactly what is going to happen. When it says, "hail," it means hail. And when it says, "fire," it means fire. Do you believe literal hail and fire fell down on Egypt during the plagues in Exodus 9? I do. However, some people who take that literally in the book of Exodus have a hard time believing something like this is going to happen in Revelation.

Hail and fire, mixed with blood, will rain down on the earth. The result is ecological disaster, but is global warming really to blame? This sounds more like a massive fire that ravages the earth, reminding me of the potential of the atomic bomb. I thank God for nuclear disarmament efforts, but nuclear weapons still exist. If some of these nuclear devices fell into the hands of terrorists, they would use them in a split second. The first trumpet announces some kind of ecological disaster, and it could be caused by nuclear holocaust.

Trumpet #2 Natural disaster: Meteorite?

> The second angel sounded his trumpet, and something like a huge mountain all ablaze, was thrown into the sea. A third of the sea turned into blood, a third of the living creatures in the sea died, and a third of the ships were destroyed. (Revelation 8:10-11)

This "natural disaster" happens upon the sea and the sea turns into blood. Whether it is some kind of red tide that floats through our oceans we don't know—but the result is devastating. Can you imagine the stench of one-third of the fish and the sea creatures dying? But why are the ships destroyed? I put a question mark here because this sounds more like a meteorite crashing into the sea. There is evidence all over our planet where meteorites have struck. I grew up in Florala, Alabama, which is located beside the largest natural lake in the state. It is perfectly round, and geologists believe it is actually a water-filled crater created by a massive meteorite long ago.

Could it be this flaming mountain coming out of the sky and landing in the sea is similar to a meteorite—but much larger? Perhaps it's an asteroid that hits the planet, and the result is a massive tidal wave that capsizes thousands of sea vessels around the globe.

Trumpet #3 Environmental disaster: Chemical warfare?

> The third angel sounded his trumpet and a great star, blazing like a torch, fell from the sky on a third of the rivers and on the springs of water. The name of the star is Wormwood. A third of the waters turn bitter and many people died from the waters that had become bitter. (Revelation 8:10-11)

During the Tribulation, a third of the earth's drinking water becomes so polluted and poisonous that no one can drink it. We often call anything falling through the night sky a "falling star," although sometimes it is not a star at all but some kind of heavenly body or meteorite. Could this "great star, blazing like a torch" be describing some sort of chemical warfare attack?

Two hundred years ago is a hiccup in the scope of world history. However, if you told people then that it would be scientifically possible to create deadly bacteria that could enter the bloodstream through human skin and kill a man, they would not have believed you. You and I know that's more than possible today. Chemical warfare has been deployed in the past, resulting in staggering casualties. We face a modern conundrum because humanity is smart enough to split the atom and create chemical weapons, but we are not good enough to be trusted with that knowledge. Scientifically, we are in graduate school, but morally we are still in preschool. Sadly, some of these disasters could result from the underside of humanity's technological advances.

Trumpet #4 Cosmic disaster: Atmospheric ruin?

> The fourth angel sounded his trumpet, and a third of the sun was struck, a third of the moon, and a third of the stars, so that a third of them turned dark. A third of the day was without light, and also a third of the night. (Revelation 8:12)

If the earth's atmosphere is filled with smoke from the raging fires of the previous judgments, a third of the brilliance of the sun could be easily obscured. Have you seen any movies that portray life in the future after a nuclear disaster? One of the first was *Mad Max;* others include the *Terminator* movies. The sun is never shining in those films, and the landscape is dark and desolate. It's interesting that even Hollywood moviemakers suspect the time is going to come in the future of widespread ruin.

In Matthew 24:21-22, when Jesus is talking about the

Tribulation, he doesn't mince words. He says, "For then there will be great distress, unequaled from the beginning of the world until now—and never to be equaled again. If those days had not been cut short, no one would survive, but for the sake of the elect those days will be shortened." What does that mean, "cut short"?

Dr. Charles Ryrie, a respected scholar, suggests a cosmic shakeup in the heavens so drastic that instead of a 24-hour day, we will have a 16-hour day. The rotation of the earth is so altered that it spins faster and our days become a third shorter than usual. You think you have trouble getting everything done in 24 hours now? How would you like to have a 16-hour day? Aren't you glad that we (the Church) are not going to be there?

More Bad News

These first four trumpets all depict compounding calamity upon the earth, but suddenly an eagle flies through the sky with more bad news. It indicates that the worst is yet to come!

CHAPTER 9

From Bad to Worse

Our culture today is disintegrating all around us. Murder, incest and crime flood the headlines of our newspapers and nightly newscasts. Have you ever wondered how God can put up with all the mess that's going on here? When is God going to punish sin? Hang on. The Tribulation is coming, and that's the time when he is going to punish rebellion. We see it unfolding before our eyes as we read through these judgments. We might call these first four trumpets the "Trumpets of War." Let's call these last three trumpets, "Trumpets of Woe." Believe it or not, things are about to get worse.

Trumpet #5 An Army from Hell

In chapter 9:1, a star has fallen. Stars are most often depicted in Scripture as heavenly bodies, but sometimes they depict angels. We know this particular star represents an angel because Scripture uses the pronoun "*he*" as having opened the Abyss (9:2). Some people think this fallen star is the devil, but God would never give Satan a key. (I wouldn't either, would you?) This is just another heavenly angel on assignment from God. This angel has a key to a pit called the Abyss where the Bible says demons reside. They are kept waiting there until the time when they will be set loose. And like hockey players in the penalty box, they are watching the clock.

Do you recall when Jesus confronted a legion of demons that were tormenting a man? The Bible says that these demons cried out to Jesus for mercy because it was not the "appointed time" (Matthew 8:29). Luke 8:31, tells us they begged him repeatedly not to send them into the Abyss. That's the same word found here in Revelation 9. The word, *Abyss* or *pit*, appears nine times in the New Testament—seven of those occurrences are in the book of Revelation. We meet this "key angel" again in Revelation 20 when Satan is put away for a thousand years:

> And I saw an angel coming down out of heaven, having the key to the Abyss, and holding in his hand a great chain. He seized the dragon, that ancient serpent, who is the devil, or Satan, and bound him for a thousand years. He threw him into the Abyss, and locked and sealed it over him, to keep him from deceiving the nations anymore until the thousand years were ended. After that, he must be set free for a short time. (Revelation 20:1-3)

Be thankful to God there are not more demons released on this earth than there are right now! Many more are held in reserve until the Tribulation to do Satan's bidding. "Isn't Satan everywhere?" you ask. No, he is not. Only God is omnipresent, and to believe Satan exists everywhere is to ascribe to him an attribute belonging to God alone. Satan is a fallen angel. He can only be in one place at one time, but his influence and his sinister organization stretches all across this planet through his demons. In the Tribulation, his demonic fleet multiplies to the nth degree.

These released demons form a veritable army, and they are so numerous that they appear as a swarm of locusts (9:3). Locusts are like grasshoppers, and they eat anything green.

A swarm can pass through a forest, leaving nothing but bare trees and devastation in their wake. John uses this picture deliberately, but it's hard for us to picture the enormous destructive potential of a locust swarm because most of us have never seen a swarm of these creatures. However, locust swarms were common in John's day. In the late 1800s in the Great Plains, settlers wrote about millions of locusts forming a cloud so dense that they covered the sky, blocking out the sun.

This demonic army also has power to inflict terrible pain like the sting of a scorpion (9:10). Scorpions have long, coiled tails with a sharp stinger containing a potent neurotoxin. When a scorpion strikes its prey, the neurotoxin attacks the nervous system. When people die from a scorpion sting, it is usually not from the venom itself. The neurotoxin causes a person's throat muscles to constrict, and often the victim chokes to death. It is a picture of the dreadful time of torture when this demonic army is released upon the earth.

Trumpet # 6 Death Angels are Released

> The sixth angel sounded his trumpet, and I heard a voice coming from the horns of the golden altar that is before God. It said to the sixth angel who had the trumpet, "Release the four angels who are bound at the great river Euphrates." And the four angels who had been kept ready for this very hour and day and month and year were released to kill a third of mankind. The number of the mounted troops was two hundred million. I heard their number. (Revelation 9:13-16)

Each of these last few trumpets escalates in severity. In this judgment, a third of the world's remaining population perishes, which is reminiscent of one of the earlier seal judgments.

This isn't the first reference to a death angel. In the Old Testament, God sent a death angel to Egypt to pass over the homes where the blood of a sacrificial lamb had been placed on the doorposts. The families that obeyed God's simple instructions were spared from the death angel because they were protected by the blood. The same can be said of those of us who have applied the blood of the Lamb, Jesus Christ, to the doorposts or entryway of our hearts.

These death angels in Revelation employ an army of 200 million. The greatest army in ancient history was the army of Xerxes of Greece, with 1.5 million soldiers. At that time, it was the most massive army in the world. In World War II, there were 16 million soldiers in the U.S. military. Can you imagine an army of 200 million soldiers? Someone has estimated an army that size would stretch one mile wide and 87 miles long. Some people say the only country that could amass an army that big is China. However, I don't believe this is a prediction about China. Instead, we need to remember that there are over 1.2 billion Muslims today. Many of them are already militant Muslims bent on attacking infidels. It's not hard to imagine that militant Muslims could easily assemble a multi-nation army that size.

According to John, the warriors look like horses (9:17-19). That's the only point of reference John had: horses and soldiers. He uses the only descriptions possible in his time. But it doesn't take much imagination to picture what he describes as the staples of modern warfare: fighter jets and cruise missiles.

> The horses and riders I saw in my vision looked like this: Their breastplates were fiery red, dark blue, and yellow as sulfur. The heads of the horses

> resembled the heads of lions, and out of their mouths came fire, smoke and sulfur. A third of mankind was killed by the three plagues of fire, smoke and sulfur that came out of their mouths. The power of the horses was in their mouths and in their tails; for their tails were like snakes, having heads with which they inflict injury. (Revelation 9:17-19)

The Reaction of the Survivors

How do you think people on earth are going to react after all these horrible judgments? Billions are dead. There is terror and darkness in the heavens. The drinking water is poisoned. Wouldn't you think that by now they would "get it" and fall on their knees and cry out to God for mercy? Think again.

We are told that they do just the opposite. "The rest of mankind that were not killed by these plagues still did not repent of the work of their hands; they did not stop worshiping demons and idols…" (9:20). God's judgment being poured out on humanity only serves to harden their hearts, and they shake their fist in his holy face!

They continue their sinful behaviors, as described in Revelation 9, many of which are the very same sins of America today—only much worse. For example, what the NIV translation calls "their magical arts" is the Greek word, *pharmakeia*—this is where we get our word, "pharmacy." In fact, "witchcraft" or sorcery in the Bible often involved the making of potions and drugs. During the Tribulation, drug abuse will escalate far beyond the already massive problem it is today. It's mind-boggling to think what it will be like during the time of tribulation when there will be a hundred-fold increase in sexual promiscuity, murder and theft throughout the entire world.

That's not to say people will enjoy being on the earth during this time. Far from it. In fact, John makes it clear they'll long to escape the devastation. However, God remains in control, preventing any form of escape. "During those days men will seek death, but they'll not find it; they'll long to die, but death will elude them" Revelation 9:6. People will desperately want to die to escape the terror, but God will not allow it. That's how terrible it is going to be.

CHAPTER 10

Bittersweet News

So far, John has been watching the events of the Tribulation unfold from the perspective of what's happening on earth. The seven seals have already been opened. The first six trumpets have sounded. In chapter 10, he begins to write again from the perspective of heaven and what is taking place there. Don't forget that the entire time he is writing this book, he is on an island in the Mediterranean Sea—exiled on the tiny island of Patmos. He has been writing and writing, and in chapter 10 it's as if God gives him a little break and speaks to him directly.

When you are writing and have a change of thought, you use a parenthesis to set it apart. That's what John is doing here in chapter 10; this parenthetical section continues halfway through chapter 11. We'll come back to the seventh trumpet when it sounds in chapter 11:15. However, for now, let's take a closer look at the strange little scene John describes about a special angel.

A Mysterious Angel

> Then I saw another mighty angel coming down from heaven. He was robed in a cloud, with a rainbow above his head; his face was like the sun, and his legs were like fiery pillars. He was holding a little scroll, which lay open in his hand. He planted his right foot on the sea and his left foot on the land,

> and he gave a loud shout like the roar of a lion. When he shouted, the voices of the seven thunders spoke. (Revelation 10:1-3)

Who is this angel robed in a cloud with a rainbow around his head? Some scholars say it is the Lord Jesus. They surmise that only Jesus can do what the angel did—stand with one foot on the sea and one foot on the earth. However, let me point out again that in Revelation, Jesus is never mysteriously veiled as an angel or any other creature. The purpose of Revelation is to reveal exactly who Jesus is, and he is *unveiled* as the Lamb of God. When I read some commentators, I feel like what the great country singer Johnny Cash said, "The Bible sure sheds a lot of light on the commentators!" I believe this is an angel, just as the Bible says from the outset in 10:1.

Angels have always interested me. That's why I wrote two books on angels. The book of Revelation has over 60 references to angels, more than any other book in the Bible except Psalms. I think it's interesting that the two books of the Bible that speak most about angels are Psalms and Revelation—the two books that also contain the most praise and more worship than in any other book.

When this angel spoke, it sounded like the roar of a lion. There were also seven thunders that "spoke." What are these seven thunders, and what did they say? We don't know because God told John not to write it down; he had John "seal it up" (10:4). Had he written it down, this would have been one more series of sevens in the book of Revelation. There would have been seven seals, seven trumpets, seven thunders, and then seven bowls of wrath.

If you read the end of the book of Daniel, you discover God also gave Daniel a prophecy that was to be sealed until the appointed time. There are some things in the Bible that have been prophesied for thousands of years but have made absolutely no sense...until today. When we read Revelation in the light of the 21st century, we can see some of the events unfolding before our very eyes on TV.

Second, the angel told John there would be no more delay. Verse 7 mentions "the mystery of God will be accomplished." What is the mystery of God? This could be referring to the mystery of evil: Why does God put up with so much evil in our world? It's a mystery to us today, but it won't always be so because the Bible says the time is coming when that mystery will be solved.

Today, we are living in the "days of delay." It is as if God's wrath against sin is being stored up, pounding against an invisible dam. At this moment, God's mercy overrides his perfect justice. Evil is rising higher and higher, but this is the time of grace. He is pleading with the whole world to accept his tender love and mercy now, because the day is coming when there will be no more delay. That's when the dam of God's wrath will burst from its confines and cover the earth.

In 2 Peter 3:3-4 we read, "...in the last days, scoffers will come, scoffing and following their own evil desires. They will say, 'Where is this 'coming' he promised?'" If you told some of the people you work with that Jesus Christ is going to come back, they might laugh at your naivety. Don't be surprised because that's how the Bible predicted they would react. Later in the same letter Peter writes, "He is patient with you, not wanting anyone to perish, but everyone to come to repentance" (2 Peter 3:9). The days of the delay of God's wrath are coming to a close, but there is still time to be saved right now.

A Bittersweet Book

After this interlude with the mighty angel, God gives John some strange instructions. He is supposed to eat the little scroll that lies open in the hand of the angel standing on the sea and land. When he tastes the scroll, it is sweet to the taste, but bitter in his stomach. There is another experience where one of the prophets of God is given directions to "eat" the Word of God. In Ezekiel 2 and 3, Ezekiel wrote a message he preached, but then he literally has to eat his own words. If all preachers had to eat their own sermons, they might choose sweeter words! When Ezekiel swallowed the papyrus upon which God's message was written, he also described the taste as bittersweet.

This is symbolic regarding the effect of God's Word in our lives. Parts of the Bible are pleasing like a sweet treat (God's promises, for example), and we love to read those passages. But along with the sweet promises, there are also passages that speak of the distasteful reality of God's judgment and wrath. For instance, as a pastor, I don't enjoy preaching on Hell. I don't enjoy writing about the wrath of God poured out during the Tribulation. It almost makes me sick to think about the terrible destiny of those who reject the love of God. However, I'm bound to declare the entire counsel of the Word of God—both sweet and bitter. Likewise, the angel prods John to continue on with his vision and get back to writing the prophecy for many people to read someday.

This must have been a great message of encouragement to John who was living in obscurity. As far as he knew, he would never get to preach again, but we are among the millions who have read his words recorded in Revelation.

The Temple in Heaven

As if eating a scroll was not strange enough, John's next instructions involve an unusual measuring rod, the temple of God and fire-breathing witnesses. Chapter 11 continues this long parenthetical pause between the opening of the sixth and seventh trumpets.

CHAPTER 11

Witnesses for God

Chapter 11 is the first reference to the three-and-a-half year period that is mentioned several times in prophecy as a midway point in the Tribulation. Daniel prophesied that the Antichrist would negotiate or confirm a seven-year peace treaty. The terms are unnamed, but many assume it will be between Israel and her enemies (Daniel 9:27). In the middle of the seven-year period (42 months), he will break the treaty and reveal his true nature, demanding that people worship an image of himself set up on a wing of the Jewish Temple.

In Matthew 24:15, Jesus spoke of this very event when he predicted that "the abomination of desolation [the Antichrist], spoken of through the prophet Daniel" would stand in the holy place (the Temple). Paul also confirms this future event in 2 Thessalonians 2:1-4. This is the Temple (that doesn't exist today, but will be rebuilt by this time) that John is told to measure. At some point in the future, the Jews will rebuild the Temple in Jerusalem and reinstate animal sacrifices.

Revelation 11:1-2 says, "I was given a reed like a measuring rod and was told, 'Go and measure the temple of God and the altar, and count the worshipers there. But exclude the outer court; do not measure it, because it has been given to the Gentiles. They will trample on the holy city for 42 months [three-and-a-half years].'"

A New Temple

The Jews have had several temples. First, they had a portable temple, a tabernacle, in the wilderness. Later, Solomon built a permanent temple, but the Babylonians destroyed it in 586 B.C. and sent the Jews into exile. After their release, they rebuilt it and called it "Zerubbabel's Temple." Herod the Great then remodeled it and it became known as "Herod's Temple," which was the temple during Jesus' ministry. In 70A.D., the Roman general Titus besieged the city of Jerusalem and destroyed Herod's Temple to spite the Jews. And the temple has never been rebuilt since that time. But this and other end-time prophecies predict that the Jewish Temple will at some point be rebuilt.

When you look at the city of Jerusalem today, there is one architectural feature that captivates the skyline—the Dome of the Rock, a blue tiled building with a beautiful golden dome. It is also called the Mosque of Omar (although Muslims do not pray there). It is the third most holy place for Muslims, behind Mecca and Medina. The legend is that Mohammed ascended into heaven from the rock under the dome (but Mohammed never even visited Jerusalem!). The Muslims captured the Temple Mount and built the dome there because it is their practice to build their shrines and mosques over the most revered sites of Jews and Christians.

In 1967, during the Six Day War when the Jews took over Jerusalem, they could have easily captured the Temple Mount as well. But they exercised restraint because they knew that if they had taken control of the Temple Mount they would have faced the outrage of millions of Muslims. Some people think that the Dome of the Rock will have to be destroyed before the Jewish Temple is rebuilt, but that isn't necessarily the case.

I've been on the Temple Mount many times, and the first thing I noticed is the Dome of the Rock is not even in the same location as the ancient Jewish Temple. The Temple was lined up exactly with the Eastern Gate (sometimes called the Golden Gate). That Eastern Gate has long been "closed" by the Muslims. It's easy to see that the Dome of the Rock is at least 50 feet south of where the Jewish Temple was located. Not only that, the street level of Jerusalem during the time of Jesus was at least 30 feet below where it is now. Layers and layers of centuries of rubble have piled up as ancient societies built on top of each other. So where will the Temple be rebuilt?

Some have suggested that the Jews are secretly rebuilding (or have even already rebuilt) a new Temple underneath the Dome of the Rock. No one can know for certain. If it were true, it would be the most closely guarded secret in the world. However, I can say for a fact that the original implements of the Temple have been replicated, and Jews with the last name of Cohen are being trained to perform the priestly functions.

The Two Witnesses

God will send two key characters into the middle of this Middle East drama that will speak on his behalf.

> And I will give power to my two witnesses, and they will prophesy for 1,260 days, [three-and-a-half years] clothed in sackcloth. These are the two olive trees and the two lampstands that stand before the Lord of the earth. If anyone tries to harm them, fire comes from their mouths and devours their enemies. This is how anyone who wants to harm them must die. These men

> have power to shut up the sky so that it will not rain during the time they are prophesying; and they have power to turn the waters into blood and to strike the earth with every kind of plague as often as they want. When they have finished their testimony, the beast that comes up from the Abyss will attack them, and overpower and kill them. Their bodies will lie in the street of the great city [Jerusalem], which is figuratively called Sodom and Egypt, where also their Lord was crucified. For three and a half days men from every people, tribe, language and nation will gaze on their bodies and refuse them burial. The inhabitants of the earth will gloat over them and will celebrate by sending each other gifts, because these two prophets had tormented those who live on the earth. (Revelation 11:3-10)

Throughout the Tribulation, these witnesses will don sackcloth and tell the people on earth to repent and turn to God. To strengthen their message, they are empowered by God to perform miracles that catch everyone's attention. Who were these two witnesses? Most Bible scholars believe they are Moses and Elijah, the same two witnesses who appeared with Jesus on the Mount of Transfiguration in the New Testament. Although Scripture does not name them here, there is supporting evidence for this conclusion.

For example, in Revelation the two witnesses are able to hold back rain for a duration of time (11:6). Elijah did the same thing for three-and-a-half years. The two witnesses turned the water into blood and brought deadly plagues on the earth "as often as they want" (11:6). Moses did that in the book of Exodus. They are able to call down fire from heaven to consume their enemies (11:5). In 2 Kings 1, we read the story of Elijah calling down supernatural fire on several delegations of King Ahaziah's soldiers when they tried to arrest him. We'll find out one day who the witnesses are for sure, but their activities bear a close resemblance to the ministries of Moses and Elijah.

For the duration of their prophesying, they are invincible. Nobody can harm them, but "when they have finished their testimony" (11:7), God allows them to be martyred. The beast (Antichrist) will be allowed to kill them. He hates these messengers and their message about God, so he does away with them. We're not told how he kills them, but we know that the people were thrilled to be rid of these two pesky preachers. When the world learns of the deaths of the two witnesses, they celebrate and exchange gifts with one another. One might say they are celebrating Anti-Christmas! It is common decency to bury somebody when they die, but these two witnesses are so despised that their corpses aren't even buried. They are left to rot in the street in Jerusalem under the watchful gaze of every people, tribe, language and nation. Until the advent of satellite television, it would have been impossible for everyone on the earth to watch a newsworthy event. But today that is entirely possible for the first time since that prophecy was written.

However, God *always* has the last word. He raises them back to life!

> But after the three and a half days a breath of life from God entered them, and they stood on their feet, and terror struck those who saw them. Then they heard a loud voice from heaven saying to them, "Come up here." And they went up to heaven in a cloud, while their enemies looked on. At that very hour there was a severe earthquake and a tenth of the city collapsed. Seven thousand people were killed in the earthquake, and the survivors were terrified and gave glory to the God of heaven. (Revelation 11:11-13)

People in California keep waiting for what they call, "The Big One." However, the largest geologic fault line on the earth is not in California. It is in Israel—the Great African Rift Valley that goes right through Jerusalem and curves into northern Africa. Jesus predicts this same earthquake in Matthew 24.

That is the end of the sidetrack in Revelation 10 and 11. We finally come to the seventh trumpet in 11:15 as the scene shifts back into heaven.

Trumpet #7 Preview of Glory

Millions of music lovers have enjoyed the majesty of George Frederic Handel's, *The Messiah*. Handel used some of *The Messiah* lyrics straight out of this text, describing a time in the future when Christ will rule the earth for a thousand years.

Many of the prophecies in the Bible relating to Jesus Christ have not yet been fulfilled. For instance, an angel told Joseph that Mary would give birth to a son named Jesus who would save his people from their sins (Matthew 1:21). However, do you know what else was said regarding the birth of Christ that hasn't been fulfilled yet? Isaiah 9:6 says, "For to us a child is born, to us a son is given, and the government will be on his shoulders." These are the very words we sing about Jesus in Handel's *Messiah*. Has that ever happened on earth? Not yet, but it will! Jesus Christ is going to set up his literal kingdom on earth for a thousand years and that is what this seventh trumpet predicts.

> The seventh angel sounded his trumpet, and there were loud voices in heaven, which said:
>
> "The kingdom of the world has become the kingdom of our Lord and of his

> Christ, and he will reign for ever and ever." And the twenty-four elders, who were seated on their thrones before God, fell on their faces and worshiped God, saying:
>
> "We give thanks to you, Lord God Almighty,
> the One who is and who was,
> because you have taken your great power
> and have begun to reign.
> The nations were angry; and your wrath has come.
> The time has come for judging the dead,
> and for rewarding your servants the prophets
> and your saints and those who reverence your name,
> both small and great—
> and for destroying those who destroy the earth." (Revelation 11:15-18)

Have the governments of this world ever been upon the shoulders of Jesus Christ? Not yet. Does the United States Congress get on their knees before they pass a bill? No. Does the British Parliament seek God's face before passing a statute? No way. The governments of this world have never been on the shoulders of Jesus, but the time is coming when Jesus will rule on earth. This amazing millennial reign is described in Revelation 20, and we will study it much more closely when we arrive there.

Don't Focus Too Much on the Future

One of the subtle dangers in studying the book of Revelation is that you can become so enamored with the future to the extent that you neglect the here and now. Some people have become so obsessed with the fourth toe on the left foot of some beast in Revelation that they never use their own feet to go out and witness for the Lord. When you study the book of Revelation, it should cause you to rejoice that your future is secure, but at the same time it should also draw your attention back to how you can reach your world for Christ today.

CHAPTER 12

Meet the Woman and the Dragon

Before John writes about the final series of seven bowls of wrath (which doesn't happen until Revelation 15), he pushes the pause button once more in chapter 12 and introduces us to some of the key characters involved in this end time drama.

> A great and wondrous sign appeared in heaven: a woman clothed with the sun, with the moon under her feet and a crown of twelve stars on her head. She was pregnant and cried out in pain as she was about to give birth. Then another sign appeared in heaven: an enormous red dragon with seven heads and ten horns and seven crowns on his heads. His tail swept a third of the stars out of the sky and flung them to the earth. The dragon stood in front of the woman who was about to give birth, so that he might devour her child the moment it was born. She gave birth to a son, a male child, who will rule all the nations with an iron scepter. And her child was snatched up to God and to his throne. The woman fled into the desert to a place prepared for her by God, where she might be taken care of for 1,260 days. (Revelation 12:1-6)

The Cast of Characters

The Woman

There is a great deal of debate about the identity of the woman described in 12:1. We're told that she is "clothed with the sun with the moon under her feet and a crown of twelve stars on her head." If you want an interesting (and sometimes comical) study, just read all the different identities ascribed to this woman in various materials. Of course, the Catholic Church insists that this woman is Mary, the mother of Jesus. However, the Christian Science religion says it is actually their founder, Mary Baker Eddy. Go figure! Some Christians even say it is the Church. I believe all of these identifications fall short of what Scripture indicates. I prefer to let the Bible interpret the Bible. When you approach the Bible that way, it seems obvious that this woman represents the nation of Israel.

Does the description of the sun, moon and stars sound familiar? In Genesis chapter 37, young Joseph had a dream where he saw the sun and the moon (which represented his father and his mother) and 11 stars (his brothers) bowing down to him. This dream became reality years later when Joseph became the Prime Minister of Egypt. Like his dream, his entire family paid homage to him. The sons of Jacob became the 12 tribes of Israel.

The Child

In John's vision, the woman is pregnant and about to give birth to a child. Verse 5 says she gives birth to a male child who will "rule all the nations with an iron scepter." This child is, without a doubt, the Messiah, the Lord Jesus Christ. The nation of Israel (the woman) indeed "gave birth" to the Lord because Jesus was of the lineage of David, the King of Israel.

The Dragon

More information is given about the dragon than either

the woman or the child. Verse 3 describes a creature straight out of a Hollywood special effects movie: "an enormous, red dragon with seven heads, and ten horns and seven crowns on his heads." Fortunately, the Bible also interprets this strange symbolism for us. Revelation 12:9 says, "The great dragon was hurled down—that ancient serpent called the devil, or Satan, who leads the whole world astray. He was hurled to the earth, and his angels with him."

The dragon represents none other than Satan himself. Many people insist the devil is just a symbol of evil—not a literal being. However, the Bible teaches there is a literal, personal devil. Jesus spoke of him (and to him!). Folklore and literature have created a caricature of the devil as a red creature with horns and a long tail, holding a pitchfork. That's not the real devil either! Don't confuse the symbols in Revelation: there is neither a real "red dragon," nor a creature in long red tights. But the devil? He is very real.

The dragon in this passage has seven heads. Heads represent the intellect or wisdom, and "seven" is the number for perfection. Satan is perfectly cunning and crafty in his attempts to cause people to disregard God and his commands. The Bible, however, is clear that he is not omnipotent (all-powerful) like God. Nowhere does Scripture indicate that he can read your mind (as some people assume). Satan isn't omniscient (all-knowing) like God. However, he is highly intelligent and we shouldn't underestimate his craftiness.

The "horns" in this symbolic creature represent military might, and the "crowns" represent political authority. The devil will promote himself in the last days through the global government of the Antichrist. The Bible says, "our struggle is not against flesh and blood, but against the rulers, against the authorities...and against the spiritual forces of evil in the heavenly realms" (Ephesians 6:12).

Heavenly World War I

Satan essentially received two demotions from the hand of God. The first time happened when Satan lost his position in heaven. I call that event heavenly World War I. Long before Creation, God kicked Satan out of heaven, and Jesus tells about witnessing this very event in Luke 10:18 when he said, "I saw Satan fall like lightning from heaven." Why did God do that? The Old Testament gives us some insight into Satan's past in Isaiah and Ezekiel, describing Satan as being a former special angel at God's disposal. Ezekiel 28:12-17 is a double-barreled prophecy: it describes God's wrath against a wicked ancient king of Tyre and also symbolically describes Satan's fall from heaven. Ezekiel was pronouncing judgment on the king, but also weaving in a word against Satan. He reveals Satan's past as an especially beautiful angel who became enamored with himself and his position as a special guardian cherub. Isaiah 14:12-14 adds even more detail about what led to Satan's initial demotion from angel to devil.

> How you have fallen from heaven, O morning star, son of the dawn! You have been cast down to the earth, you who once laid low the nations! You said in your heart, "I will ascend to heaven; I will raise my throne above the stars of God; I will sit enthroned on the mount of assembly, on the utmost heights of the sacred mountain. I will ascend above the tops of the clouds; I will make myself like the Most High."

Although Satan was cast out of heaven long ago, he still

retains access to God today. We know that Satan has access to God because of what we learn in Job 1. In Job, Satan presents himself before God. When God asked him where he had been, Satan reported that he had been "roaming" throughout the earth. The Bible describes him as an angry, roaring lion, prowling around and looking for someone to devour (1 Peter 5:8). So, he has access to God, but he has been kicked out of heaven. And he is not happy about it.

The Devil's Diabolical Plan

We read in 12:4, "The dragon stood in front of the woman who was about to give birth, so that he might devour her child the moment it was born." It has always been the intent of Satan to destroy Jesus. Throughout the earthly life of Jesus, the devil tried to kill him prematurely, starting when he was just a small child. The devil inspired Herod the Great, who sent the order to slay every male child in Bethlehem two years old and younger. The king understood from prophecy that a rival to his throne (Jesus) was born there.

When he began his earthly ministry, the religious leaders began plotting Jesus' death long before Calvary. When Jesus preached in his home synagogue in Nazareth, the Bible says the leaders took him outside the city and were going to cast him off a cliff. Satan was attempting to destroy the Messiah again, but Jesus walked through the crowd unharmed—it wasn't yet time for him to die. And Satan entered into the heart of Judas to betray Jesus. I suspect that when Jesus was nailed to the cross, the devil squealed with delight—he thought he had secured a victory. But three days later, he knew that he had failed!

Heavenly World War II

John informs us that there will be another spiritual struggle in heaven between Satan and God's agents. I call this conflict Heavenly World War II. Spiritual warfare ensues as Michael (the archangel) and his angels fight against the dragon (12:7-9). The great dragon was overpowered and hurled down to the earth. In the first conflict, Satan lost his position as an angel. In this future conflict, he will lose access to God's presence. At that, he takes one-third of the angels with him, as described in 12:4. The stars swept out of the sky by the dragon's tail in verse 4 are not literal stars. We've already seen that a star can be a symbol of an angel—good or bad.

As verse 12 explains, losing his "key card" to heaven's gates ignites the devil's fury. He "knows his time is short" because God is about to take care of evil once and for all at the end of Revelation. In the meantime, he will take out his anger on God's people, according to 12:17.

So where is Satan right now? Jesus said Hell was prepared for the devil and his angels, but he is not there yet. He is busy misleading people and nations on earth, which is why Paul called him "the god of this age" (2 Corinthians 4:4). The Bible describes him in 12:10 as "the accuser" and, because he still retains access to God's presence, he spends all of his time now accusing God's children in front of God. That's what Satan did in regards to Job. He proposed that the only reason Job praised God was because he was so blessed. But, the devil said, if God took away Job's blessings he would certainly curse God. Of course, that was not the case.

It will be a great day in the future when Satan will lose his access to heaven, and he can no longer accuse believers

(Tribulation saints). However, for the present time, accusation is an essential part of his satanic strategy: to accuse you of how dirty, filthy and rotten you are. If you are a Christian, but you feel burdened with shame all the time, you will be ineffective in your witness for Christ. You play right into the devil's hand at that point because your guilt nullifies the power of the Gospel. If you're not sure deep down that you're forgiven, it makes it difficult for you to tell anyone else about the mercy and grace of Christ.

An Important Distinction

Many Christians have a hard time distinguishing between the Holy Spirit's conviction and satanic accusation. There is a tremendous difference between the two. First, the Holy Spirit *never* convicts you of sin you've confessed and put under the blood of Jesus. If there is some sin you've committed in your past and you've confessed it to Jesus for forgiveness, you may feel guilty about it later. But that is not the Holy Spirit talking; it is the devil accusing you.

Second, the Holy Spirit is always specific when he convicts you of sin. You won't just have a general sense of guilt; the Holy Spirit will convict you of a certain act or thought you need to confess and make right. The devil, on the other hand, burdens you with feelings of constant guilt and shame. He whispers that you can never experience forgiveness.

Third, the Holy Spirit always points you toward the solution when you make a mistake: confession and cleansing. He guides you to confess your sin and be set free. Whereas the devil accuses you and makes you feel hopelessly dirty and shameful. Do you see the difference? The devil is the accuser of the brethren, and the Holy Spirit convicts. The devil is the D.A. who is always trying to say you are guilty before God, but thank God we have an advocate with the Father, the Lord Jesus Christ. He stands before the Judge and says, "It's true. He or she a sinner, but I have forgiven all their sin."

A Strategy to Fight the Devil

The Tribulation saints overcome the devil's schemes with a specific strategy. Chapter 12:11 says, "They overcame him by the blood of the Lamb and by the word of their testimony; they did not love their lives so much as to shrink from death." When you plead the blood of Jesus Christ, Satan trembles and flees. Genesis 3:15 contains the first Messianic prophecy in the Bible. God makes a prediction about the animosity between the "seed of woman" (Jesus) and the devil. God puts a curse upon the serpent and upon man and woman. He says to the devil, "You shall bruise his heel, but the seed of woman shall crush your head!" When Jesus died on the cross and shed his blood, he stomped on the head of the serpent. Satan was mortally wounded. He's still hanging around, but his doom is sure.

Whenever you suffer from the devil accusing you of old, past sins try this. Say, "Satan, my sins have been placed under the blood of Jesus Christ." Say it out loud to him. *Wait, isn't that praying to the devil?* No, you're not praying to a cat when you tell it to "Scat!" Just rebuke him and overcome him by pointing to the blood of Jesus.

These Tribulation saints also gave testimony about the truth of God's Word and Jesus' work in their lives. Likewise, Christians need to give their testimony to other people. You need to hear it—and Satan needs to be reminded—that you are saved, forgiven and secure forever.

Finally, the Tribulation saints also overcame the devil because they didn't "love their lives so much as to shrink from death" (12:11). In other words, when given a choice between death or forsaking Jesus, they chose death. Throughout history, the blood of the martyrs has been the seed of the Church. If we were asked if we'd be willing to die for the cause of Christ, most of us would answer, "Yes." But that's because we know we likely won't be asked to die for Christ. Are you willing to live for him and love him more than life itself? When you aren't afraid of death, you neutralize one of the devil's most effective weapons.

Protection for Israel

> When the dragon saw that he had been hurled to the earth, he pursued the woman who had given birth to the male child. The woman was given the two wings of a great eagle, so that she might fly to a place prepared for her in the desert, where she would be taken care of for a time, times and half a time [three-and-a-half years] out of the serpent's reach. Then from his mouth the serpent spewed water like a river, to overtake the woman and sweep her away with the torrent. But the earth helped the woman by opening its mouth and swallowing the river that the dragon had spewed out of his mouth. Then the dragon was enraged at the woman and went off to make war against the rest of her offspring—those who obey God's commandments and hold to the testimony of Jesus. (Revelation 12:13-17)

Have you ever wondered why the Jews have always been such a persecuted people? Why did Pharaoh try to limit their numbers and keep them enslaved? Why did Hitler try to provide "the final solution to the Jewish problem"? Why do so many countries vehemently hate Israel today? Satan has always been behind the persecution against Israel since time began, and in the last days it's only going to grow worse. However, at a certain point God is going to supernaturally rescue a remnant of Jewish believers in Israel and keep them "out of the serpent's reach." John mentions the "wings of great eagle." He had no other frame of reference, but this could be a military airlift. God will hide them away in a "prepared place" somewhere in the desert.

Just when the dragon (the devil) thinks he has these believers in his grasp, they get away. And that unleashes his fury once more. He will send a flood of soldiers in his satanic-inspired army after them—but like Pharaoh's army being swallowed up in the Red Sea, the earth will open up and engulf them in what appears to be a tremendous earthquake.

The Biography of the Beast

In chapter 13 of Revelation, we are given more details about the Antichrist, the beast who leads this attack against God's people. Revelation is not the first or only time we learn about the Antichrist in the Bible. What do we know about him? Is he alive today? In the next chapter, we will trace his roots all the way from the Old Testament and dissect his sordid history in what I call: the biography of the beast.

CHAPTER 13

A Demonic Duo

The world will be in a state of initial panic after millions of Christians have mysteriously vanished from earth in the Rapture. Imagine the ramifications of this worldwide phenomenon on the stock market and banking system, as millions of portfolio-owners no longer exist! Thousands of planes will be pilotless, and thousands of ships will be captainless and crewless—bringing travel, commerce and trade to a standstill. Christians serving at all levels of infrastructure, including the U.S. military, police forces, medical facilities, local and national governments, educational institutions—will all be gone. Looting and crime will skyrocket around the world. The remaining leaders will be scrambling to bring this global chaos under control.

Against this backdrop of unprecedented mass turmoil, one leader will appear as the voice of reason to unite everyone into a one-world economic and political system of control. He and his right hand man, the false prophet, will head the world's affairs as the ultimate "demonic duo." What do you get when you cross Satan and an ambitious politician? The Antichrist. He will have such charisma and persuasive power that when he talks, the whole world is going to listen.

The Beast from the Sea

> And the dragon stood on the shore of the sea and I saw a beast coming out of the sea. He had ten horns and seven heads, with ten crowns on his horns, and on each head a blasphemous name. The beast I saw resembled a leopard, but had feet like those of a bear and a mouth like that of a lion. The dragon gave the beast his power and his throne and great authority. One of the heads of the beast seemed to have had a fatal wound, but the fatal wound had been healed. The whole world was astonished and followed the beast. (Revelation 13:1-3)

When the Bible says this beast (the Antichrist) "came from the sea," it's not talking about a saltwater creature. The word picture of the "sea" is symbolic of him rising out of the tumultuous waves of chaos that wash over the world during the Tribulation. This context is clarified in Revelation 17:15: "Then the angel said to me, 'The waters you saw, where the prostitute sits, are peoples, multitudes, nations and languages.'"

The Bible says in 1 John 2:18 "...you have heard that the antichrist is coming, even now many antichrists have come. This is how we know it is the last hour." An antichrist (small "a") is anyone who is against or "anti" Christ and what he represents. That's why John says there are many antichrists who have come and gone through the years. However, the capital "A" Antichrist is a unique being with a strategy for world domination so evil it can only be described as satanic.

Beastly Behavior

It's no mistake that John describes him as a "beast" because, contrasted to the vision of Jesus the Lamb, this is a hideous creature. "Beast" has nothing to do with his physical appearance; it's his conduct that reveals a beastly nature. The physical features John describes are not literal, but symbolic clues to the behavior of the Antichrist.

This beast has similar features to the dragon in chapter 12. The seven heads represent perfect wisdom (although he doesn't use his wisdom for good; instead, he is perversely cunning). The "ten crowns on his horns" represent a ten-nation confederation that will support him in the Tribulation. John then gives three pictures of what the beast resembled, using terminology from his first-century perspective, mixed with prophecy from the book of Daniel.

If you know Bible prophecy, these three images ought to be familiar: a leopard, a bear and a lion. In the book of Daniel chapter 8, Daniel sees the same three animals. Note that John reverses the order from Daniel who described a lion, a bear and then a leopard. One reason for this difference may be because Daniel is looking *forward* to a period in time when he sees these creatures. In a sense, John is looking *backwards* at these empires.

Daniel's prophecy symbolized three great world powers that were to come on the scene afterwards. The leopard is the representative of the Greek dynasty under Alexander the Great. Alexander the Great was as swift as a leopard in the way he conquered foreign lands. In fact, some historians say he died at the age of 33 of a broken heart because there were no more worlds to conquer. The bear is the Empire of the Meads and the Persians. Whereas Alexander moved swiftly to conquer lands like a leopard, the Meads and Persians lumbered along, methodically conquering kingdoms. The lion represents what we believe to be the Roman Empire, a regal dynasty. Like Daniel's prophecy, there's something about this Antichrist that reminds John of the character of the great Grecian dynasty, the Meads and the Persians and even the Romans.

A Fatal Wound

What really attracts the world's attention to the Antichrist is his miraculous recovery from receiving a "fatal wound." This reference appears three times in this chapter. It could be that the Antichrist is going to be injured in some way, maybe even killed, and revive!

Satan is the great imitator of God. As such, he has tried to replicate (in his limited way) everything good God has ever done. Therefore, it is not surprising that Satan is going to revive the Antichrist from the dead, much as Jesus was resurrected from the dead. (The difference being, of course, that Jesus is alive forevermore and the Antichrist would be resuscitated only to eventually die again.)

If the world saw a world ruler assassinated on live television and then a week or two later saw him come back to life, don't you think that person would attract some attention? It would be as if John F. Kennedy suddenly came back on the world scene after his assassination in 1963. Most every American alive today has at least seen footage of his assassination and funeral procession. What if, and this is pure speculation for the sake of illustration, JFK came back from the dead? What if he went on national television and said, "Thanks to the miracle of cryogenics, I have been healed and I am alive again." Don't you imagine he would be an amazingly popular world figure? (If you dare say that I said JFK is the Antichrist, you've missed my point.) I'm just saying that if something like that happened, every nation on earth would be astonished.

Worldwide Worship of the Beast

There are many references to the Antichrist in the Bible other than Revelation. Paul says, "Don't let anyone deceive you in any way, for that day [the Second Coming] will not come until the rebellion occurs and the man of lawlessness is revealed, the man doomed to destruction" (2 Thessalonians 2:3). This "man of lawlessness" is the Antichrist. What does he do that is so terrible? It's what Jesus warned about: the "abomination that causes desolation." It's when the Antichrist is going to set himself up in the Temple in Jerusalem and demand the world worship him.

And that's exactly what Revelation 13:4 says happened. "Men worshiped the dragon because he had given authority to the beast, and they also worshiped the beast and asked, 'Who is like the beast? Who can make war against him?'" Satan's desire has always been to be worshiped. Remember, the reason he lost his position in heaven is because he wanted to be like God (Isaiah 14:14). Satan took Jesus to the top of a mountain to give him a panoramic view of all the kingdoms of this world that could be his—if only Jesus would worship him. When people worship the beast, they will in fact be worshiping Satan.

But don't think he's going to be successful in his plans for worldwide adoration. In 2 Thessalonians 2:8, Paul writes, "And then the lawless one will be revealed, whom the Lord Jesus will overthrow with the breath of his mouth and destroy by the splendor of his coming." That's what Jesus is going to do to the Antichrist when he comes back—Jesus will far outshine the Antichrist as the true King worthy of worship. "The coming of the lawless one will be in accordance with the work of Satan displayed in all kinds of counterfeit miracles, signs and wonders, and in every sort of evil that deceives those who are perishing. They perish because they refuse to love the truth and be saved" (2 Thessalonians 2:9-10). The Bible says Satan will enable the beast to counterfeit miracles, signs and wonders to give the appearance of God-like qualities. However, those who fall for it will perish because they do not look to the one true God and his Son, Jesus Christ.

Blasphemies, Blasphemies

> The beast was given a mouth to utter proud words and blasphemies and to exercise his authority for forty-two months [three-and-a-half years]. He opened his mouth to blaspheme God, and to slander his name and his dwelling place and those who live in heaven. He was given power to make war against the saints [the Tribulation saints] and to conquer them. And he was given authority over every tribe, people, language and nation. All inhabitants of the earth will worship the beast—all whose names have not been written in the book of life belonging to the Lamb that was slain from the creation of the world. (Revelation 13:5-10)

The Antichrist is so vehemently opposed to God and his followers that he will blaspheme his name and go after those who choose to follow him (the Tribulation saints). He is even going to blaspheme the believers who are already in heaven with God—those who were caught up with Jesus at the Rapture. I imagine he will engineer some sort of logical explanation regarding those who disappeared at the Rapture to downplay God's work. He will tell the rest of the world to be thankful that all the "fanatical" Christian conservatives are long gone.

The False Prophet

The other half of this demonic duo, the false prophet, will help spread propaganda that the world is better off without the Christians. "Good riddance!" he will say to explain the strange phenomenon regarding millions of missing persons. Unlike the "beast from the sea," the Bible describes this false prophet as the "beast from the earth," meaning "land" or "dirt." When the Bible speaks of "the land," it is usually a reference to Israel, God's Promised Land. This could be a sign that the false prophet is going to come out of the nation of Israel. He will exercise the authority of the beast, much like his Vice-President. He does not want to be worshiped. But at his direction, all the inhabitants of the earth will worship the beast.

To make his case for worshipping the beast, the false prophet will have the power to perform miracles. Not all miracles are from the hand of God. In the Old Testament, even Pharaoh's servants were able to perform some miraculous wonders. One of the miraculous signs is the false prophet's ability to cause "fire to come down from heaven to earth in full view of men" (13:13). Some have suggested that could be a reference to a nuclear bomb explosion.

Once he has the attention of the entire world, he turns their focus to "an image in honor of the beast" (13:14). This image was given the power to breathe and talk, John says. When you read the word "image," you may think of a statue, but the word simply means a picture. In verse 15, John is amazed to discover that the image can talk. Try to visualize what he saw two thousand years ago and describe it with a limited first-century vocabulary. Now, think about this description in 21st century terms. I wonder if any of you reading this have an image that "talks" to you in your home? Those with flat screen televisions may have one of these images hanging on the wall in your living room right now. All John saw was a talking head, perhaps broadcast worldwide on television. This talking head orders everyone, "You must now worship me! I am your God!"

He Controls Commerce

Now we've come to a portion of Scripture you have likely heard but never fully understood.

> He [the false prophet] also forced everyone, small and great, rich and poor, free and slave, to receive a mark on his right hand or on his forehead, so that no one could buy or sell unless he had the mark, which is the name of the beast or the number of his name. This calls for wisdom. If anyone has insight, let him calculate the number of the beast, for it is man's number. His number is 666. (Revelation 13:16-18)

This false prophet is going to require everyone to have some kind of number or code on their hand or their forehead in order to buy or sell goods. One hundred years ago, that kind of technology did not exist. However, I carry a number with me on a credit card that enables me to purchase goods anywhere I go. If I don't get approval for that purchase using my number, I am not allowed to buy it. In a real sense, the credit card manufacturers control what I can and cannot purchase.

You may remember when a clerk at the grocery store punched in all of the prices of your groceries by hand. Today, merchants easily scan bar codes to make your purchases.

Many believe this convenient technology could be the

basis of what this passage describes. Many banks are putting pictures on credit cards as a form of identification. The next step beyond putting your picture on the credit card is putting the credit card on you! You already know identity theft is a huge problem when credit cards are lost or stolen. But what if your unique number was on you, imperceptibly imbedded under the skin of your hand or forehead? That would make it so easy, right? You wouldn't have to carry a purse or wallet anymore in this cashless society. When you walked into a store they could just scan you and your purchase!

The only way a monetary system of exchange like that can work, of course, is if everybody participates. The false prophet and the Antichrist are going to *make* people participate in this program for their own good. If they don't participate, they can't buy. They can't sell. And they cannot eat! People who refuse to take the mark of the beast will be vehemently persecuted.

The Number of the Beast

If you study eschatology as much as I have, you'll almost burst out in laughter to read all the fantastic interpretations of the number of the beast, 666. I've read how people try to count the letters in a person's name and transpose the letters and numbers in a twisted game of mathematical gymnastics in their attempt to calculate the number 666. Once again, the key to understanding this number is given in the verse itself. It is simply the number of man. Man was created on the sixth day; he labors for six days and rests on one. In Gematria, six is the number for a human being. In comparison, seven is the number of perfection (God). The number "six" repeated three times (three is the number of divinity) is a futile attempt on the part of a human being trying to be perfect like God. It's a 666 (imperfect human) trying to be a 777 (divine perfection) but falling short. As Roman 3:23 confirms, "All have sinned and fallen short of the glory of God."

Man will never be God, as much as he wants to be like him. The Antichrist will get closer than anybody else, but the best even he will ever do is 666. Hollywood script writers have blown this number out of proportion as if it's some sort of secret satanic code. It's no secret at all—when the world sees a man stand up and claim to be God (777), those who know the truth of God's Word will realize he is the one Scripture warns us about.

CHAPTER 14

Pleas from the Angels

During the Tribulation, there is a group of people who will not take the mark of the beast. They are the 144,000 Jews we first met in Chapter 7. While the Antichrist and the false prophet are spreading their evil doctrine, these 144,000 Jewish evangelists are passionately pleading with people to come to Jesus Christ for salvation.

> There before me was the Lamb, standing on Mount Zion, and with him 144,000 who had his name and his father's name written on their foreheads. And I heard a sound from heaven like the roar of rushing waters and like a loud peal of thunder. The sound I heard was like that of harpists playing their harps. And they sang a new song before the throne and before the four living creatures and the elders. No one could learn the song except the 144,000 who had been redeemed from the earth. These are those who did not defile themselves with women for they kept themselves pure. They follow the Lamb wherever he goes. They were purchased from among men and offered as firstfruits to God and the Lamb. No lie was found in their mouths; they are blameless. (Revelation 14:1-5)

Throughout history, many religious groups have claimed to represent this 144,000. Most notably are the Jehovah's Witnesses. Their founder claimed at the beginning of the cult that there would be only 144,000 "true believers" and adherents to their religion. Once they enlisted 144,000 Jehovah's Witnesses in the world, then God's kingdom would come. (The only problem is there are now far more than 144,000 Jehovah's Witnesses in the world today, and Jesus still has not returned!). John gives us more insight into the true identity of this group.

The Mysterious 144,000

This passage in Revelation 14 jumps ahead to describe the honor this group will receive after the Tribulation is over. John describes these men as sexually pure—they remained celibate and did not marry. The Apostle Paul, although he had the right to be married, chose instead to be single so he could be more effective at preaching the Gospel. Of course, there is nothing wrong with being married. However, throughout history, there have been special saints who have chosen not to marry so they could devote all their time to God's work and "follow the Lamb wherever he goes" (14:4).

This zealous group of believers in Jesus became a thorn in the side of the Antichrist because they opposed everything he did. They insisted on telling people the truth about God. The Antichrist and all of his followers had his mark upon their foreheads, but these Jewish evangelists had the name of the Lamb and his Father on their foreheads. John pictures the 144,000 singing to the Lord in grateful praise for preserving them throughout the Tribulation.

The Pleas of the Angels

John then sees four angels, and each one of these angels has a specific message to share with those left on the earth.

> Then I saw another angel flying in midair, and he had the eternal gospel to proclaim to those who live on the earth— to every nation, tribe, language and people. He said in a loud voice, "Fear God and give him glory, because the hour of his judgement has come. Worship him who made the heavens, the earth, the sea and the springs of water." (Revelation 14:6-7)

Angel One: Judgment has come!

The voice of the first angel gives a word of warning—judgment has come! We read throughout the Bible about the fact that one day God will pour out his righteous judgment upon the wickedness and sin of humanity. "Judgment is coming," say the churches today. This angel announces that judgment is no longer "coming"—in fact, it's here! His job is to proclaim the "eternal gospel" to everyone, everywhere. In effect, he is the world's last missionary, and he shouts this final plea with a sense of urgency: Fear God!

What is the Gospel? Sometimes you'll hear a preacher who yells about hellfire and brimstone. When he finishes, some people wipe their brow and say, "Man! He really preached the Gospel!" Well, not necessarily! He might have just helped people get ready for the Gospel because the Gospel is the "good news," not just the bad news by itself. The good news is not so good without the bad news.

Imagine if I said to you, "Good news! Your house is *not* on fire." You'd look at me like I was crazy. But what if I prefaced that news with the fact that I'd just seen two fire trucks racing down the street towards your neighborhood. Knowing that *your* house is not the one on fire would be good news because of the bad news about a fire. The backdrop of the good news of the Gospel must always be the bad news of reality, which is that we are sinful people who cannot help ourselves.

Judgment is coming. But God has offered us a way to escape this judgment, and it is through his Son, Jesus Christ. Condemnation for sin is coming, but if you are a believer, it is not coming your way! "There is no condemnation for those who are in Christ Jesus" (Romans 8:1).

Angel Two: Babylon is fallen!

In Revelation 14:8, a second angel announces that Babylon has fallen. What is Babylon? Babylon is the key subject of chapters 17 and 18, and we will study it more in depth at that point. For now, just understand that Babylon is not a place. It's a system. It represents the totality of the worldly economic and religious system of the Antichrist. This angel announces, "Fallen! Fallen is Babylon." Why does he say it twice? We're going to see in those later chapters that both religious Babylon and economic Babylon are going to collapse. This devastating worldwide event is going to happen just before Jesus returns for the Final Battle.

Angel Three: Escape God's wrath!

> A third angel followed them and said in a loud voice: "If anyone worships the beast and his image and receives his mark on the forehead or on the hand, he, too, will drink of the wine of God's fury, which has been poured full strength into the cup of his wrath. He will be tormented with burning sulfur in the presence of the holy angels and of the Lamb. And the smoke of their torment rises forever and ever. There is no rest day or night for those who worship the beast and his image, or for anyone who receives the mark of his name." This calls for patient endurance on the part of the saints who obey God's commandments and remain faithful to Jesus. Then I heard a voice from heaven say, "Write: Blessed are the dead who die in the Lord from now

> on." "Yes," says the Spirit, "they will rest from their labor, for their deeds will follow them." (Revelation 14:9-13)

All through history, God's fury has been diluted, mixed with his mercy and his unfathomable love. We could not survive God's wrath if it were not tempered with his mercy. But the time is going to come in the future where "his wrath will be poured full strength." All those who have refused to accept Jesus Christ as their Lord and Savior will suffer eternal torment. Remember, God never intended any person to go to Hell. Jesus confirmed in Matthew 25:41 that Hell was prepared for the devil and his angels. But those who reject the mercy of God will end up there. God doesn't send people to Hell; they send themselves because of their refusal to accept his provision through Christ.

Some think Hell is going to be one great party with other sinners like themselves. However, the Bible is clear in Revelation 14:11 that there is no rest day or night for those who rejected Christ and worshiped the beast. There is going to be a constant sense of tension in Hell: no rest, no peace, no tranquility.

The word "hell" is the Greek word *gehenna*, which was a reference to the Valley of Gehenna outside Jerusalem. This valley had a loathsome reputation as the site of ancient pagan worship involving human sacrifice. The deep, narrow ravine eventually became the local city garbage dump. It burned night and day, and the putrid smoke from the smoldering animal carcasses and other trash rose high into the air. This is the picture Jesus paints of the constant fire and torment in Hell. It is nowhere near the picture some people have in their minds of Hell being an eternal nightclub with all their "sinner" friends. Others think, "Well, if there is a Hell, at least I'll get it over with quickly!" I'm afraid not. Chapter 14:11 says, "…the smoke of their torment rises forever and ever."

But there is a beautiful contrast in verse 13 of this same chapter. "Blessed are the dead who die in the Lord...they will rest from their labor." Isn't that good to know? The Bible says those who know the Lord when they die will enter a time of rest for them "and their works will follow them." Your good works do not send you to heaven, but they do *follow* you to heaven.

Angel Four: Reap the harvest!

> I looked, and there before me was a white cloud, and seated on the cloud was one "like a son of man" with a crown of gold on his head and a sharp sickle in his hand. Then another angel came out of the temple and called in a loud voice to him who was sitting on the cloud, "Take your sickle and reap, because the time to reap has come, for the harvest of the earth is ripe." So he who was seated on the cloud swung his sickle over the earth, and the earth was harvested. Another angel came out of the temple in heaven and he too had a sharp sickle. Still another angel, who had charge of the fire, came from the altar and called in a loud voice to him who had the sharp sickle, "Take your sharp sickle and gather the clusters of grapes from the earth's vine, because its grapes are ripe." The angel swung his sickle on the earth, gathered its grapes and threw them into the great winepress of God's wrath. They were trampled in the winepress outside the city, and blood flowed out of the press, rising as high as the horses' bridles for a distance of 1,600 stadia. (Revelation 14:17-20)

The message of the fourth angel is a word to the other angels to reap the harvest. When I was a young boy in

Alabama, a company called International Harvester made the most popular pieces of farm equipment. This angel is describing a literal international harvest of the entire earth, and the "crop" they are harvesting is all the unrighteous people. God's angels will be sent to the four corners of the earth to do their work.

In Matthew 13, Jesus told the story of a man who planted wheat in his field. However, his enemy slipped in that night and planted weeds among the wheat. As the wheat began to grow, the weeds also began to grow, and the stark contrast between the two was obvious. The farmer's servants offered to pull up all the weeds, but he wisely said no. He would let them both grow together until the harvest, and then his workers would separate the weeds and the wheat. He would take the weeds and burn them in a fire.

We don't have to wonder what Jesus was talking about in this parable because he gave the interpretation (13:36-43). He says the Son of Man is the farmer who plants good seed (the children of God), but the devil has slipped in and planted weeds (the unrighteous) among them. So, when the harvesters come, they separate the weeds from the wheat.

In this passage in Revelation 14, the unrighteous "weeds" are described as grapes, ripe for harvest. The weeds in Jesus' parable are thrown in the fire; in Revelation, the grapes are thrown into God's winepress and trampled. The blood that flows out of the winepress spreads to the depth of a horse's bridle for about 180 miles (the approximate length of the nation of Israel, north to south, where the Final Battle takes place). Jesus continues in Matthew 13, "The harvest is the end of the age, and the harvesters are angels. As the weeds are pulled up and burned in the fire, so it will be at the end of the age. The Son of Man will send out his angels, and they will weed out of his kingdom everything that causes sin and all who do evil. They will throw them into the fiery furnace..." (13:39-42).

A Safe Place to Stand

Uncontrollable prairie fires ravaged the property and homes of many early settlers across the Midwest. It was not unusual to see the horizon filled with smoke as a fire rushed by prairie winds threatened to overtake their homes. Many families lost their farms and their homes until they learned how to battle the fire. Whenever they saw a wildfire coming toward them, they set the area around their house on fire in a controlled burn. Then, the families could stand inside the burned out area around their homestead, and the fire would not harm them. Likewise, the only place to safely escape the wrath of God's judgment is to stand where his judgment has already fallen. God's wrath fell upon his Son on the cross because the Bible says Jesus carried all our sin. Therefore, the ground around the cross has already been "burned" by his holy fury 2000 years ago. The only safe place where you and I can stand to escape his wrath is at the foot of the cross where his judgment has already fallen.

CHAPTER 15

Our God Saves

We've been watching what takes place on the earth with the beast and false prophet for a few chapters. Now, the first part of chapter 15 describes a scene back in heaven. It reminds me of watching a football game on television. Throughout the game, the broadcast switches between the view on the field and the commentators in the booth.

The Crystal Sea

In the opening of chapter 15, John is looking at a supernatural sea that is so beautiful and unusual that it seems to be made out of glass, mingled with soft, flamed tongues of fire. Standing beside this sea is a whole host of people who have been victorious over the Antichrist. They are the Tribulation saints, those who persevered to the end during the Tribulation and did not take the mark of the beast. This group "sang the song of Moses, the servant of God, and the song of the Lamb" (15:3).

The Song of Moses

In Exodus 15 after Moses led the children of Israel across the Red Sea, the Israelites sang a song of celebration. Its lyrics comprise the first song recorded in the Bible. It's rather long, but here is an excerpt from Exodus:

> The enemy boasted, "I will pursue, I will overtake them.
> I will divide the spoils; I will gorge myself on them.
> I will draw my sword and my hand will destroy them."
>
> But you blew with your breath, and the sea covered them. They sank like
> lead in the mighty waters. Who among the gods is like you, O LORD ?
> Who is like you— majestic in holiness, awesome in glory, working wonders?
> You stretched out your right hand and the earth swallowed them.
> In your unfailing love you will lead the people you have redeemed.
> In your strength you will guide them to your holy dwelling. (Exodus 15:9-13)

The children of Israel sang about their victory over Pharaoh, and the Tribulation saints will sing of their victory over the Antichrist. A relentless enemy hotly pursued both and God protected and provided for each group.

The Song of the Lamb

The other song they sing is, "The Song of the Lamb." Notice the differences and the similarities between these two songs. They were both sung beside a sea. The song of Moses was first sung beside the Red Sea; the song of the Lamb is sung beside the crystal sea in heaven.

They were both sung after a time of great victory. The children of Israel had victory over Pharaoh, and the Tribulation saints have victory over the Antichrist. They were both sung for the same reason. Like the Israelites, the Tribulation saints were brought through and out of a time of testing and they overcame.

Notice also that the song these Tribulation saints sing is full of praise and admiration toward God. They don't boast anything about themselves. They don't pat themselves on the back for their faithfulness during the Tribulation. They don't extol their own ability to persevere. It's all about God.

Notice the second person pronouns in Revelation 15:

> Great and marvelous are *your* deeds. Just and true are *your* ways.
> Who will not fear *you*, O Lord,
> and bring glory to *your* name?
> For *you* alone are holy.
> All nations will come and worship before *you,*
> for *your* righteous acts have been revealed. (Revelation 15:3-4)

There are two kinds of songs Christians sing in church. One is a song of testimony, including hymns like, "I Have Been Redeemed" or "When The Roll Is Called Up Yonder, I'll Be There." That's a testimony about what something that has happened as a result of God's presence in our lives. The other kind of praise song is a song sung directly to the Lord. The song the Tribulation saints sang, the Song of the Lamb, was this kind of praise song. One is sung about Jesus; one is sung to him.

Seven Angels File out of the Temple

The next thing John sees is the temple in heaven, which he refers to as the tabernacle of the Testimony (15:5). Seven angels come out of the temple, dressed in brilliant linen with gold sashes around their chests. Even though they're dressed in white, they are assigned a dirty job—pouring out the bowls of God's wrath on the earth in chapter 16.

CHAPTER 16

The Last Plagues

We've seen the seven seals, the seven trumpets, and now it is time for the last and final series of God's wrath—seven bowls of wrath. I have to warn you—these last seven plagues are so gruesome and devastating, it is hard to believe the people on the earth can take much more.

The Last Seven Plagues

Bowl #1 Cancer of the skin

The first bowl of wrath, the first judgment, is some sort of cancer of the skin (16:2). Apparently, painful sores and boils will break out on the people all over the earth. It will be sickening to watch as millions of people are disfigured with these boils. Part of this could be as a result of the fallout from a nuclear holocaust, leaving radiation sores on the skin of the survivors. These boils have similarities to what we've seen in both the trumpets and the seals and also to the plagues during the time of Moses in Exodus.

Bowl #2 Contamination of the sea

The second angel poured out his bowl on the sea, and it turned the color of the sea as red as blood (16:3). The result was the death of millions of sea creatures—everything from the tiniest starfish to the massive blue whales strangle on this blood-red contaminant. In 1949 on the western coast of Florida, they experienced an ecological phenomenon that scientists called "the red tide." Billions of red venal flagellates bonded together for a 60-mile stretch of water. The water appeared blood red, and all the fish and sea creatures in that area died and washed up on the shore. Can you imagine if all the oceans of the world experienced some kind of grand-scale environmental disaster that killed every living sea creature?

Bowl #3 Corruption of the streams

The third angel poured out his bowl on the freshwater rivers and springs, and they appeared like blood, too. The first recorded miracle Jesus performed was that of changing water into wine. If God-in-the-flesh could turn water into wine, he can certainly turn water into blood. John says, "Then I heard the angel in charge of the waters say: 'You are just in these judgments, you who are and who were, the Holy One, because you have so judged; for they have shed the blood of your saints and prophets, and you have given them blood to drink as they deserve.' And I heard the altar respond: 'Yes, Lord God Almighty, true and just are your judgments'" (16:5-7).

There seems to be a sense of poetic justice here. It's as if God says to the bloodthirsty culture on earth, "You want blood? I'll give you blood…to drink." The U.S. is the number one exporter of violence around the world through our media. "Blood and guts" rule in our music and in our movie theaters, and we call it "entertainment." A time is coming in the future when the world will see no end to the blood.

God demonstrates this perfect sense of justice throughout Scripture by following human bloodshed with more blood.

For example, Pharaoh drowned all the boy babies born to the nation of Israel in an attempt to suppress the Hebrew people who were growing in numbers. How did Pharaoh himself die? He drowned. That's the justice of God. In the book of Esther, Haman devises an evil plot to build gallows on which to hang his Jewish enemies. How did Haman die? He hung on those same gallows, another example of the poetic justice of God. God told King Saul to kill all the evil Amalekites and destroy their influence on God's people, but Saul didn't do it. Guess who then one day killed Saul? The Amalekites.

Bowl #4 Catastrophe of the sun

The fourth angel poured out his bowl on the sun, which caused it to intensify its rays and actually scorch the planet and the people. In Luke 21: 25, Jesus confirms that there will be "signs" in the sun, moon and stars during the Tribulation. In Revelation 8:12, we read about another solar catastrophe where part of the sun was supernaturally darkened.

Our outer atmosphere (the ionosphere) serves as a filter blocking out the sun's harmful rays. This layer of particles prevents us from frying to a crisp from the tremendous heat emitted by the sun, which is a raging fireball of gases. Scientists have been warning us for years that we are depleting the protective ozone layer. What would happen to our planet if there were nothing to block out the harmful rays of the sun? On an ordinary day, SPF 540 would not be enough to protect people from being terribly sunburned.

This passage might also describe the effects of a massive solar flare. Solar flares are tremendous explosions on the surface of the sun. One of the largest recorded flares in 1859 smothered about two-thirds of the earth's skies with a blood-red aura. This caused many to think it was the end of the world! In 1989, a smaller flare occurred and, as a result, took out power stations in Canada. Scientists have the capability today to analyze future solar flare conditions, and they have some significant predictions of solar flares in the near future. In Revelation, we see a forecast more accurate than what scientists can predict. The future solar catastrophe the Bible predicts will be unprecedented, and it will be devastating to our fragile planet.

You would expect that sinful humanity would reach their limit of enduring this judgment, fall on their knees and cry, "God, save us!" It's hard to believe, but Revelation 16:9 says they will steadfastly refuse to do any such thing. They will actually curse God's name instead. There seems to be no limit to how much people can harden their hearts against God.

Bowl #5 Darkness for the beast

The fifth angel poured out his bowl on the throne of the beast and plunged his kingdom "into darkness" (16:10-11). God alone has power over worldwide darkness and light. The same God who merely said at the beginning of Creation, "Let there be light" can just as easily call sudden, supernatural darkness into play. The nation of Egypt experienced an eerie supernatural darkness during the plagues in the time of Moses. When Jesus was hanging on the cross at noon, it became as dark as midnight for three hours as Jesus took on the sins of the world. On May 19, 1780, history records an entire day of unusual darkness over New England and parts of Canada—so dark that candles had to be used from noon onward. Although the Antichrist will appear to be in charge during the Tribulation, God demonstrates in this fifth bowl that he has the power to plunge the throne of the Antichrist into darkness at any time. In verse 10, we see there will be such incredible misery from the darkness and lingering pain from the other plagues that the inhabitants of earth will gnaw their swollen tongues and curse God.

Bowl #6 Demonic enemies

In the sixth bowl of wrath, we see the unholy trinity of the devil (the dragon), the Antichrist (the beast) and the false prophet at work. Evil spirits that appeared as frogs come out of their mouths and speed throughout the earth to summon kings to the great Final Battle against Israel.

> The sixth angel poured out his bowl on the great river Euphrates, and its water was dried up to prepare the way for the kings from the East. Then I saw three evil spirits that looked like frogs; they came out of the mouth of the dragon, out of the mouth of the beast and out of the mouth of the false prophet. They are spirits of demons performing miraculous signs, and they go out to the kings of the whole world, to gather them for the battle on the great day of God Almighty. (Revelation 16:12-14)

Right now, there are several nations who are desperate to destroy Israel and wipe this tiny country off the map. In the Tribulation, it will not take too much convincing to summon them to the Battle. On their way there, they would have to cross the Euphrates; the angel prepares their way by drying up its waters.

You may recall back in Revelation 9 that four angels were bound at the Euphrates awaiting a specific time when they would be released to summon an army of 200 million to kill one-third of the earth's inhabitants. In Revelation 16, we see that the longest river in Southwest Asia has been dried up so as not to impede their progress as they stealthily march toward Israel. Today, there are reports that the Euphrates is already drying up because of drought and misuse from neighboring countries. It is significantly smaller than it was just a few years ago; in 2009, some experts estimated it was almost half the size it used to be. This sixth bowl is not only a plague that dries up a once mighty river; it is foreshadowing a great battle to end all battles.

Throughout the Word of God, it has been prophesied there will be a climatic final battle between the nations when God absolutely destroys wickedness and sets himself up as ruler over all. This is popularly referred to as the Battle of Armageddon, but the battle will actually take place in Jerusalem according to Zechariah 14 where the Antichrist has set up his "image" in the Temple. The Bible clearly says that the armies of all the nations will *gather* at a place called Armageddon before advancing to Jerusalem to launch the battle.

As popular as the term "Armageddon" has become in our culture, you would think it would be referenced many times in Scripture. Actually, Revelation 16:16 is the only time this word is mentioned. Therefore, notice that it is not referenced in Scripture as the "Battle of Armageddon." In Hebrew, the first part of the word "Armageddon" is actually *Har*, which means "mountain" or "hill." *Megiddo* is an ancient city in central Israel. Put the words together and you will see that "Armageddon" literally means "the hill of Megiddo." If you look on a Bible map, you can easily find the plain of Jezreel, which is located at Megiddo. This is a beautiful valley about 45 miles north of Jerusalem—a perfectly flat staging area for this multi-nation army to gather. We will study the details of this climactic battle when we get closer to the end of the book of Revelation.

The Promise

Before we get to the final bowl of God's wrath, we find some good news. In the midst of this final series of horrible judgments, God gives a promise. Remember, the original recipients of this letter were the seven churches in Asia Minor. Since that time, Christians throughout the ages have been reading the book of Revelation, and these words in Revelation 16:15 have given them comfort.

God interrupts the chronology of the storyline with a timeless personal message from his Son, Jesus. He says, "Behold, I come like a thief! Blessed is he who stays awake…" Then he describes a man who keeps his clothes beside his bed ready to go out into the night at any moment, lest he be exposed.

In a similar passage in Matthew 24:43, Jesus said, "If the master of the house had known when the thief was coming, he would have been ready." In 1 Thessalonians 5:2, Paul writes that the Day of the Lord will come like a thief. After my father died, my mother was living alone in Mobile, Alabama, and one night someone broke into her house and stole a lot of her belongings. However, I know for certain that if my mother had known when that thief was coming (or better yet if I had known when that thief was coming!) every police officer in Mobile, Alabama would have been parked outside our house. We would have been ready for him! In the same way, we need to be prepared for and anxiously anticipating the return of Christ.

Bowl # 7 Destruction of Babylon

> The great city split into three parts, and the cities of the nations collapsed. God remembered Babylon the Great and gave her the cup filled with the wine of the fury of his wrath. Every island fled away and the mountains could not be found. From the sky huge hailstones of about 100 pounds each fell upon men. And they cursed God on account of the plague of hail, because the plague was so terrible. (Revelation 16:19-21)

The seventh angel pours out the final bowl of wrath and a loud voice from the temple announces, "It is done!" Lightning, rumblings, thunder and a severe earthquake ensue—an earthquake unlike any other in the history of the world. Verse 19 describes the great city (Jerusalem) splitting into three parts in the wake of this disaster. In Zechariah, the Bible describes the same scene at the Final Battle:

> I will gather all the nations to Jerusalem to fight against it; the city will be captured, the houses ransacked, and the women raped. Half of the city will go into exile, but the rest of the people will not be taken from the city. Then the LORD will go out and fight against those nations, as he fights in the day of battle. On that day his feet will stand on the Mount of Olives, east of Jerusalem, and the Mount of Olives will be split in two from east to west, forming a great valley, with half of the mountain moving north and half moving south. (Zechariah 14:2-4)

So, is the mountain going to be split into two or three parts? Zechariah says "split in two," while Revelation 16 says Jerusalem (which is on a mountain) was split into "three parts." The answer is: it's both. The Kidron Valley already separates the mountain into two parts today, dividing the

Mount of Olives from the city of Jerusalem proper. When Jesus comes to fight the Battle and sets his mighty foot on the Mount of Olives, that mountain will then split in two, making three parts from one great city.

Plague number seven ushers in what is called "the destruction of Babylon." In ancient times, Babylon was both a country (modern day Iraq) and a city. However, as I indicated earlier, it symbolizes much more in the plot of Revelation. Babylon represents the totality of the Antichrist's world system that has been in operation throughout the Tribulation. Now that we're moving toward the climax of the book, we see that time has run out on Babylon. What John sees next is so strange and perplexing that an angel is sent to help interpret what he is seeing.

CHAPTER 17

Religious Babylon

In the opening verses of chapter 17, John sees a woman riding a beast, but she is not a woman at all. She represents the world system of "Babylon"—every ounce of human pride, ingenuity and self-reliance that utterly and totally rejects God. This mindset will encompass every nation on earth to a heightened degree in the Tribulation.

> One of the seven angels who had the seven bowls came and said to me, "Come, I will show you the punishment of the great prostitute, who sits on many waters. With her the kings of the earth committed adultery and the inhabitants of the earth were intoxicated with the wine of her adulteries." Then the angel carried me away in the Spirit into a desert. There I saw a woman sitting on a scarlet beast that was covered with blasphemous names, and had seven heads and ten horns. The woman was dressed in purple and scarlet, and was glittering with gold, precious stones and pearls. She held a golden cup in her hand, filled with abominable things and the filth of her adulteries. This title was written on her forehead:
>
> MYSTERY
> BABYLON THE GREAT
> THE MOTHER OF PROSTITUTES
> AND OF THE ABOMINATIONS OF THE EARTH.
>
> I saw that the woman was drunk with the blood of the saints, the blood of those who bore testimony to Jesus. When I saw her, I was greatly astonished. (Revelation 17:1-6)

If you saw a vision that disturbing, "greatly astonished" might not fully describe your reaction. You might run away screaming! So, what is the meaning behind this strange scene? Fortunately, the angel quickly interprets what John saw, detail by detail.

Fallen Kingdoms

First, let's start with the beast the woman is riding. John is confused by what he saw, so he asks the angel to explain it to him. But the answer the angel gives seems to be even more confusing, at first glance! You may have to read this passage in 17:7-14 several times to understand it, so let me help you unpack what the angel says.

The beast has seven heads (again, a perfectly cunning strategy) that represent seven kings. According to 17:9-10, "The seven heads are seven hills on which the woman sits. They are also seven kings." The angel goes on to say that five of these kingdoms had "fallen." In fact, history records the rise and fall of five great ancient kingdoms: the Egyptian Kingdom, the Assyrian Kingdom, the Babylonian Kingdom, the Persian Kingdom and the Kingdom of Greece. Those five had already fallen when John had this vision, so that information would have made sense to him.

The sixth kingdom that "is" (meaning present day for John) was the Roman Kingdom, and John was all-too-familiar with it because he had been punished and exiled under the wicked Roman Emperor, Domitian. The angel indicates there would be one more kingdom in the future, which some believe could be the Holy Roman Empire (Europe under the influence of the Roman Catholic Church). The eighth is the

Antichrist's government. We'll learn later that the hub of his religious operations is in one city, and the rest of its command center is in another unnamed city.

The ten crowns represent ten nations who together form the beast's global cabinet. Daniel also prophesied that during the time of the Antichrist there would be ten kings who gave him power and ruled with him. For years, some scholars suggested these ten countries would be the European Union, but now there are well over ten nations in the EU. Another possibility is that these ten nations could represent a coalition of the ten most powerful Muslim nations, including Saudi Arabia, Iran and Pakistan. Several years ago, ten of the leading Muslim nations formed an economic consortium for trade agreements between their nations. Considering the fact that about 22% of the world's population was Muslim in 2010, this even more powerful future coalition would exercise enormous control over world affairs. The angel says this confederation has one purpose—to give power and authority to the beast and make war against the Lamb (Jesus Christ).

The Origin of Babylon

"Babylon" comes from the word, "Babel." In Genesis 11, the people in ancient Babylonia boasted that they could build a tower high enough to reach God. In Hebrew, *Bab* means "gate." *El* means "God." They were literally trying to build "the gate to God" by their own wisdom and skill. That is the essence of the philosophy behind the Babylon system: getting ahead without God.

Of course, God looked down and said, "Well, I'll just do something about that." Zap! Suddenly the workmen were all speaking different languages, and they could no longer understand one another to build the tower. So, they separated into the nations of the earth. But do you know "the rest of the story"? According to legend, the ringleader in the building of the tower of Babel was named Nimrod. The Bible briefly mentions Nimrod and identifies him as the great-grandson of Noah. He was a great hunter and leader who established a kingdom in Babylon (Genesis 10:9-12).

According to the ancient document called the *Gilgamesh Epic*, Nimrod and his wife, Simiramis, had a son named Tammuz. The ancient legend said Tammuz was killed by a wild boar. However, after his mother wept over his body for 40 days, he miraculously came back to life. When this happened, the people were amazed and worshipped Simiramis and her son, giving birth to a new pagan religion. In fact, from this legend came the idol, the "queen of heaven" described in Jeremiah 44:19, who was worshipped by some of God's own people!

This was not a God-sanctioned religion, but a false religion that focused on "mother and son" worship. This cultic practice spread throughout ancient civilization. In fact, every ancient civilization has a similar myth regarding a mother goddess who gave birth to a child god. The Phoenicians called her Ashtorath, and her son's name was Baal. The Egyptians called the mother Isis, and her son was Osiris. The Greeks called her Aphrodite, and her son's name was Eros. The Romans named the mother goddess Venus, and her son's name was Cupid.

This cultic mother-son religion developed into a specific liturgy of ceremonies and practices. In the spring of the year, they would worship this "risen god" for 40 days before the vernal equinox—weeping, fasting and praying to memorialize the death of Simiramis' son. God called the prophet Ezekiel's attention to the fact that some women, the very children of God, had been swept up in observing this tradition of weeping for Tammuz (Ezekiel 8:14). At the end of the 40 days in this cultic religion, the feast of Ishtar was observed to celebrate his resurrection, and they worshipped both mother and son. As part of this ancient cultic practice, they used "holy water" and ate wafers served by their celibate priests. Many of the women became "vestal virgins," women so committed to their practice of religion that they would never marry.

Can you think of a world religion today that worships a mother and her son? And does the practice of observing 40 days of fasting sound familiar? It should, because parts of this cultic religion's traditions were also adapted into one of the world's most popular and powerful religions. The roots of the mother-and-son worship worked their way into what became known as the Roman Catholic Church.

A History Lesson

How did this happen, you ask? When John wrote Revelation, the Romans were in charge, but there was no Roman Catholic Church. For the first 300 years of the early Christian Church, the Church was persecuted terribly by the Roman Empire. However, in the year 313, the Roman Emperor Constantine had a vision before going into battle. He said he saw written in the sky these Latin words, *In hoc signo vinces*, which means, "By this sign, conquer!" and he saw a cross. This was an amazing religious experience for Constantine, and he concluded he would fight "in the name of the cross" by painting a cross on the front of his army's shields.

After an amazing victory over his enemy, he issued a decree that legalized Christianity. Unfortunately, in his zealous efforts to legalize Christianity, he actually paganized Christianity. The beautiful Bride of Christ (the Church), only 300 years old, was forced into a marriage with the popular pagan Roman culture. Unfortunately, the pure Church then adopted many of the pagan religious practices and Christianized them into the establishment of the Roman Catholic system. In the future Tribulation, the religious system in charge will be paganized to an even higher degree—and the Antichrist will use religion to his advantage.

The Woman on the Beast

That's where John's future vision of the woman riding the beast ties in with this little history lesson. The angel spells it out for John and says this woman riding the beast isn't a real woman at all. She represents the apostate religious system of Babylon, which was full of false teachings. She (the religious system) will form an alliance with the beast, a political mastermind.

Now we understand that the Antichrist has a dual agenda: it is both a religious and economic strategy. He uses one to aid the other, but at the same time the woman is using the beast like a rider uses a horse to further her cause as well. She is, after all, the "mother of abominations" (17:5). ("Abomination" simply means spiritual or religious sin.) She and the beast are working together. This false religion and the Antichrist are teammates.

What is the False Religion?

We know this false religion during the Tribulation is centered in a great city. The angel explains in 17:18, "The woman you saw is the great city that rules over the kings of the earth." So, what city and what false religion are we talking about? Here is one more clue: the seven heads of the beast she is riding represent "seven hills." One of the major cities in the world fits the description and is known as the city on seven hills: Rome. The Roman Catholic Church is, of course, centered in Rome.

Lest you think I am into Catholic-bashing, let me clarify. Am I saying that the Roman Catholic Church is somehow of the beast? Absolutely not! Many people today in the Roman Catholic Church believe in Jesus and the Bible more than they do their church traditions. I think born-again Roman Catholics will be raptured with other believers. That said, it is the Roman Catholic *system* of promoting teachings and traditions that are not in the Bible that will become the ripe breeding ground for a future amalgamation of one false super-religion that the whole world will willingly adopt as the truth. It's a system that will include Romanism, but it is much bigger than that during the Tribulation. This religion will be a mixture of the occult, humanism, Romanism and a sprinkle of New Age—and millions will tout it as the best religion ever invented. This passage in chapter 17 shows us the Antichrist is going to use this powerful, worldwide religious *system* to promote his agenda for a while.

There is already a movement in our world for ecumenism or the development of a one-world, universal church. There are a lot of liberal Protestants who would gladly jump in with the Roman Catholic Church today to make that happen.

By this time in the future, all the church systems will be united into a One-World Church based in Rome. This mega-religious center will absorb all the other denominations left behind after Jesus raptures the believers.

Recognizing Religious Babylon

So, now you understand the woman is a symbol of a false religious system called Babylon. The angel gives John a series of clues to confirm the identity and location of this false system of religion. It's undeniable that the Roman Catholic system as it exists today has an alarming similarity with how the angel describes this future false religious system.

False Teaching

He says of the woman, "She is the mother of prostitutes and of the abominations of the earth" (17:5). A false religion is like a prostitute in that it "sells out" to lies and is no longer pure. It's a case of spiritual adultery. For example, some of the doctrines of the Roman Catholic Church involving Mary are nowhere to be found in Scripture and more closely resemble the mother-and-son worship of ancient paganism.

For instance, the doctrine of an Immaculate Conception claims Mary was born without sin. Most Protestants (and many Catholics) believe that the immaculate conception refers to Jesus being born without sin—but the Roman Catholic Church teaches *Mary* as being sinless and pure. They also claim Mary was a perpetual virgin—meaning, she was a virgin before Jesus' birth and remained so throughout her life. The Bible clearly says she was a virgin before Jesus was born but that he had half-siblings. (Joseph was their father; God was Jesus' Father.)

They also teach the bodily assumption of Mary. This Roman Catholic doctrine teaches that Mary never died; instead, she ascended into heaven just like Jesus did. Therefore, she is called the "co-mediatrix" with God in the Roman Catholic Church. According to their beliefs, Jesus is the mediator and she is the co-mediatrix.

There are five main Catholic basilicas in Rome. I have been in St. Peter's Basilica on the square of the Vatican and seen one of Michelangelo's sculptures called "The Madonna," also called "The Pieta." It is a sculpture of Mary holding the body of Jesus after he has been taken down from the cross. It is a very tender, touching sculpture because Mary is weeping and holding her son in her arms. If you measure that sculpture to scale, Mary is so much larger than the adult Jesus. If Jesus were six feet tall, then according to that sculpture, Mary would be over nine feet tall. Michelangelo didn't make a miscalculation; he was just reflecting the Roman Catholic Church's belief that Mary is larger than life (and larger than Jesus!). In another basilica called The Cathedral of St. Mary's, over the front portico hangs a life-size crucifix. On one side of the crucifix, Jesus is crucified, but on the backside of the same cross Mary is seen crucified.

Political Alignment

There is another clue given in Revelation 17:2 about how this false religious system operates. It says, "With her the kings of the earth committed adultery and the inhabitants of the earth were intoxicated with the wine of her adulteries." This woman (false religion) is involved with world governments and is politically involved. Only one system of religion has its own embassy that sends out ambassadors. The Vatican in Rome is a country recognized by the United States and possesses a seat in the United Nations.

Great Wealth

So now we know she is centered in Rome, involved in world politics and, according to 17:4, she possesses great wealth. "The woman was dressed in purple and scarlet, and was glittering with gold, precious stones and pearls. She held a golden cup in her hand." The Roman Catholic Church controls trillions of dollars in assets throughout the world, mostly in real estate and banking. The Vatican museum alone owns art worth many billions of dollars. If you ever visit the Vatican museum, you will be amazed at the thousands of priceless pieces of art. And at any one time, only ten percent of the Vatican's art is on display!

Involved in Persecutions

This religious system is also guilty of persecuting Christians. Verse 6 tells us, "I saw that the woman was drunk with the blood of the saints, the blood of those who bore testimony to Jesus." Certainly the Roman Catholic Church has never persecuted Christians, right? Read your history books. When I took church history, my professor called it, "The Period of the Pornographic Popes." It was a time during the Dark Ages when nobody was reading the Bible, especially the Roman Catholics or the Popes. They were involved in criminal activities and sexual immorality to the hilt.

Martin Luther could not stomach the selling of indulgences, essentially selling people a ticket to heaven. He sparked the Protestant Reformation when people began to rebel against the Roman Catholic Church. When the people began reading the Bible for themselves and discovered the truth of God's Word, the Pope lost power. And he didn't like it.

Thus began one of the darkest times in history known as the Inquisition. Tens of thousands of believers were killed by the leaders of the Roman Catholic Church. Tomas de Torquemada, who was called "The Inquisitor General," was the bloodiest of all. The day Pope Sixtus IV granted his title, his gift to the Pope was the heads of 2,000 so-called rebellious Christians. Will history repeat itself in the Tribulation? The Bible indicates a future false religion will be behind a lot of the persecutions of Tribulation saints who refuse to take part in the Antichrist's plans.

Betrayed by the Antichrist

The last clue the angel gives about this false religious system is it will be betrayed by the Antichrist. Surprise—the "horse" she is riding will buck her off! God won't have to destroy religious Babylon; the Antichrist will do it for him. Revelation 17:16 says, "The beast and the ten horns that you saw will hate the prostitute. They [meaning the Antichrist and these other kings] will bring her to ruin and leave her naked; they will eat her flesh and burn her with fire."

Any good politician uses all his allies to their advantage, and this is exactly what the Antichrist does. He will use this apostate religious system to establish his world domination, but the time is going to come when he will no longer need religious Babylon. He will no longer want to share his power, so he will turn on it and destroy it.

Ultimately, the Lamb will overthrow both the beast and the woman. Revelation 17:14 says, "They will make war against the Lamb, but the Lamb will overcome them because he is Lord of lords and King of kings—and with him will be his called, chosen and faithful followers."

Fall of Economic Babylon

In the next chapter, there are fewer symbols to understand as we learn about how the economic system of the Antichrist begins to topple next. Up until now, we've seen the Antichrist getting more and more powerful, but the tide is turning against him.

CHAPTER 18

The Fall of Babylon

In 2008, our nation began struggling in a recession that many are comparing to October 24, 1929, when the New York Stock Exchange crashed. On that one day, it lost 12.8% of its value, which led to the Great Depression. Many lost their jobs and even committed suicide because of that economic collapse. Many people remember what happened on October 19, 1987 when in one day the Stock Market fell 22.6%, losing 560 billion dollars on paper. On October 6, 2008, the Stock Market started another weeklong decline in which the Dow Jones Industrial Average fell 1,874 points or 18.1%. This pattern of devastating loss is just another painful reminder that our economic system is rather fragile. However, the entire world will experience a final, unprecedented economic collapse toward the end of the Tribulation.

An Economic System Doomed to Fail

Our world is definitely moving toward a unified economic system with one universal currency. Doing business in another country is often complicated by the fluctuating exchange rates between currencies, which is one of the reasons why many countries in the European Union have adopted the euro as their currency. Revelation indicates that the world will adopt a universal currency under the leadership of the Antichrist. Ultimately, however, this unified economic system (that looks so brilliant on paper) will fail. Why?

First, this economic system is doomed to fail because it is demonic at its core. Anything Satan touches is tainted with failure. The angel mocks the self-proclaimed "Babylon the Great" and says:

> Fallen! Fallen is Babylon the Great! She has become a home for demons and a haunt for every evil spirit, a haunt for every unclean and detestable bird. For all the nations have drunk the maddening wine of her adulteries. The kings of the earth committed adultery with her, and the merchants of the earth grew rich from her excessive luxuries. (Revelation 18:2-3)

Earlier in the book of Revelation, we saw Hell is going to be opened and hundreds of thousands of additional demons are going to scatter over the earth like vultures seeking prey. The angel compares this flock of demons to "every unclean and detestable bird." When you read the parables of Jesus, birds sometimes symbolized the work of Satan. For example, in the Parable of the Sower, birds ate the seed the farmer scattered so that it could not grow. When Jesus interpreted that parable, he compared the birds to Satan who takes away the seed (the Word of God) so it will not grow. A system controlled by tremendous demonic influence is doomed to fail from the start. It cannot go up, up, up when God says it's going down, down, down.

Another reason this economy collapses is because the leadership behind it will make costly mistakes. The angel says all the nations "have drunk the maddening wine" of this enormous economic conglomerate. It seemed like such a wonderful system initially that everybody who bought into it became drunk on it. An inebriated person loses his or her sense of judgment and the ability to decipher right and wrong.

In fact, the angel points out that those in power abused their positions. Only one class of people became wealthy as a part of this economic system—those in power. Don't think the Antichrist's economic system is a *fair* system. This one-world economic system will not benefit several classes. It creates two classes: the incredibly rich and those living in poverty because they are enslaved to the system. For example, in Mexico, Central America and South America, there are two classes of people: the very wealthy and those living in poverty. Likewise, there are economists who say a similar gradual elimination of the middle class is going to happen in America and Europe.

Bucking the System

Another angel pleads for people to reject the philosophy of the day and turn to God instead. He issues this call to the Tribulation saints who dare to be different and not follow the worldwide throng of people enamored with the beast.

> Then I heard another voice from heaven say: "Come out of her [meaning, the Babylon system], my people, so that you will not share in her sins, so that you will not receive any of her plagues; for her sins are piled up to heaven, and God has remembered her crimes. Give back to her as she has given; pay her back double for what she has done. Mix her a double portion from her own cup. Give her as much torture and grief as the glory and luxury she gave herself. In her heart she boasts, 'I sit as queen; I am not a widow, and I will never mourn.' Therefore in one day her plagues will overtake her; death, mourning and famine. She will be consumed by fire, for mighty is the Lord God who judges her." (Revelation 18:4-8)

As God has always done, he tells his people to separate and come out from among the rest of the world to follow him. And many will do so, at a great cost—even their lives. These are the Tribulation saints we've been studying who accept Christ in a time when the world is at an all-time high of wickedness and evil.

Collapsing under the Weight of Sin

Archeologists estimate the tower of Babel was likely a ziggurat reaching 600 feet high—nowhere near reaching heaven. What finally does reach the threshold of heaven though is the pile of sins accumulated over seven years by "Babylon the Great"! And God remembers each one, the angel says. Take note—the Bible says God will forgive your sins and "remember them no more" when you confess them to him and repent (Jeremiah 31:34). He takes confessed sins and puts them as far as the East is from the West (Psalm 103:12). However, the same God who forgets forgiven sin says he always remembers unconfessed, unforgiven sin. All the sins of the wicked people in this world system pile up to heaven during the Tribulation.

According to Revelation, those who are caught up in this worldly, godless system have been living on borrowed time, stacking up immorality like firewood. But their precarious charade is going to come crashing down, God says. And when it does, it will happen swiftly. Everything they've earned and achieved will come to ruin.

Millions will be devastated by the total collapse of this economic system, especially the merchants who are in charge of trade. As it was during John's time, most of the world's cargo is still shipped by sea because it's the cheapest way to move large amounts of goods. At an undetermined time in the latter half of the Tribulation, the economic meltdown will take place. The first to go will be the goods shipped overseas. In Revelation 18:11-13, it lists cargo typical for that day, but take a closer look. Listed there among the silver and silk are human souls! Revelation says the time is coming when a soul and a body are put on the same value level as other commodities. The only thing the Antichrist and his economic system consider valuable is the bottom-line. Lenin accepted that he would have to destroy millions of people in order for communism to be accepted. However, to him, it was worth the price.

To the satanic system that rules the world during the Tribulation, a soul is worth absolutely nothing. It bothers me that we are moving closer to that callous stance every day. Our nation has come to the point where we say an unborn baby is nothing but a mass of tissue.

But not God—to Jesus, a soul is of infinite worth and value. The Bible says God leaves the 99 and goes searching for that one lost sheep, one lost person. Jesus Christ said, "What shall it profit a man if he gains the whole world, and loses his soul?" (Mark 8:36).

An Unidentified City

At the fall of Babylon, many will weep on earth over what they have lost—but many will rejoice in heaven because the end is near! Revelation 18:20 says, "Rejoice over her, O heaven! Rejoice, saints and apostles and prophets! God has judged her for the way she treated you." All of heaven rejoices because God is avenging all the Tribulation saints who were martyred during the Antichrist's heyday. To illustrate his point, the angel accompanying John picks up a giant boulder and tosses it into the sea to demonstrate how, just like that, the great "city of Babylon" that serves as a command center for the Antichrist will be gone from sight. This city's cultural prominence, its beauty and its wealth are all going to disappear from view as if it never existed, and rejoicing will break out in heaven.

We don't know which city it is now, but during the Tribulation one city will rise to the place of economic superiority—then it will fall. Since the sea captains seem to be able to see the city burning from their ships (Revelation 18:17-18), that suggests a city on or near the coast.

Hallelujahs in Heaven

In verse 1 of chapter 19, the party continues when a great multitude in heaven begin shouting "Hallelujah!" The word *hallelujah* means "praise the Lord," which appears throughout the Old Testament. However, *hallelujah* appears in the New Testament only four times, and all four instances are in chapter 19. All of heaven rejoices at the awe and majesty of God because his perfect plan for the world is finally going to be put into motion. Revelation 19 is my favorite chapter in Revelation after all of the doom and gloom because God is about to put an end to all the evil in the world.

CHAPTER 19

The Real Hallelujah Chorus

Sometimes people have a faulty interpretation of the Bible that I call "Star Wars" theology. Star Wars is a classic tale about good versus evil where the good side of the Force is battling against the dark side of the Force. As the movie unfolds, it's impossible to tell which side is going to win in the end. Finally, in a nail-biting conclusion, the good side of the Force wins (much to the relief of the Luke Skywalker fans)… but the victory comes only by a narrow margin.

Some uninformed Christians envision a similar kind of cosmic struggle going on between God and Satan in Revelation, as if it's a real close match! By the time they reach this point in Revelation, they think the game is tied with two minutes left. However, the story in Revelation isn't a cliffhanger. It's not even a fair fight.

All throughout the Bible, we're told that God will be victorious in the end. You can go all the way back to Genesis 3 where God predicted exactly what would happen when he said the "seed" of Eve was going to crush Satan's head. The Final Battle is over before it even begins. Jesus conquered the devil at Calvary 2000 years ago. That's why you don't need to fear the devil, even though the Bible describes him as being like a roaring lion. At Calvary, Satan was rendered a big toothless and clawless cat. All he has left is his roar.

When I was a kid, I used to read a series called the Hardy Boys mystery books before I went to sleep. Some nights I'd read past my bedtime, engrossed in the story. My mother would come in and tell me to turn out the light and go to bed immediately. But I didn't want to stop reading because inevitably Joe and Frank Hardy would be in the middle of a dangerous crisis. They might be tied down to a conveyor belt with a buzz saw about to kill them! I couldn't stand the suspense of not knowing what happened, so sometimes I'd flip to the last page to find out if they survived. It was always a relief to read on the last page something like, "After returning home, Joe and Frank sat down to a nice dinner with their family." I didn't know the details, but I could close the book and turn out the light, confident that in the end everything was going to be okay. The same is true for God's Story. When it seems there's no way out of the trials and struggles you go through, you ought to look on the last page of this Book and realize that everything works out in the end.

The majority of Revelation is not a pleasant story. From chapter 6 to chapter 18, John describes the time of terrible tribulation during which the wrath of God is poured out upon the earth. The seven seals were broken, the seven trumpets were blown, and the seven bowls of wrath were poured out. When I come to chapter 19, I want to sigh with relief! The focus is no longer on the judgment that takes place on earth but on the celebration taking place in heaven because God is victorious over evil!

The Real Hallelujah Chorus

In Revelation 19:1, there is a great chorus in heaven that shouts, "Hallelujah!" This is the *real* "Hallelujah Chorus" by George Frederic Handel. Most of us have never heard the entire oratorio, *Messiah*, because it is an enormous composition. We usually hear a section of it at Christmas, or we might be familiar with certain movements. Handel wrote the entire piece in 24 days. He hardly ate and scarcely slept as he composed non-stop. The result was a beautiful musical interpretation of God's plan of salvation through the sacrifice of Jesus Christ. A wealthy friend, Charles Jensen, gave Handel a libretto (the text of a composition like an opera) based on Jesus' life, which he took entirely from the Bible. Then Handel set the text to music.

When the *Hallelujah Chorus* was performed in the presence of the King of England in 1743, the king was so moved that he rose to his feet during the first few notes. The rest of the audience obliged, spawning a tradition we still follow today when the *Hallelujah Chorus* is sung. We don't stand in honor of Handel; we don't stand in honor of the music; we stand to honor the "Lord God Omnipotent." As moving as the *Hallelujah Chorus* is on earth, can you imagine what it is going to be like in heaven when the real King of Kings and Lord of Lords receives our praise?

In 1869 in Boston after the Civil War, our nation held a celebration called "The Peace Jubilee." A 10,000-voice choir and a 1,000-piece orchestra performed for tens of thousands of people—all unamplified. The high point of the opening concert of the five-day celebration undoubtedly was the "Anvil Chorus. " Fifty firemen pounded anvils and artillery cannon fired in synchronization, accompanied by church and cathedral bells. It was so successful that Europe hosted a World Peace Jubilee a few years later with twice the number of choir and orchestra members! Talk about raising some noise! But that is *nothing* compared to the worship that is going to take place in heaven as Christians from every tribe, nation and tongue gather around the throne. John says the multitude praising God was so great they sounded as if he were standing under the Niagara Falls rush of mighty waters, accompanied by the loudest peals of thunder human ears had ever heard!

The Bride and Groom

The whole purpose of the worship and celebration is in honor of a wedding about to take place. Revelation 19:7 tells us who is getting married: "Let us rejoice and be glad and give him glory! For the wedding of the Lamb has come, and his bride has made herself ready." The Bride is the Church, and the Groom is Jesus Christ, the Lamb.

I love weddings. I've always enjoyed performing them. When I'm performing a wedding and the organist begins to play the wedding march, every head turns to look at the bride entering the room. But after glancing at the bride, I always turn to look at the groom. I love to see his reaction when he looks up the aisle and sees his bride walking toward him. In an American wedding, everyone looks at the bride, but at this heavenly wedding, the focus is going to be on the *Bridegroom*—Jesus!

The Church is the Bride of Christ, meaning New Testament believers. However, there will be other people who are invited to the wedding feast. I don't think Old Testament believers like Jacob or Moses or Abraham will be a part of the Bride. They will be at the wedding feast as friends of the Bridegroom. Jesus makes this distinction when he says, for example, that John the Baptist was a "friend" of the bridegroom.

A One-of-a-Kind Wedding

Revelation 19:7 says, "The bride has made herself ready." How does the Church do that? In answer to that question, let me explain a Jewish wedding. In Western/American weddings, we generally have an engagement, followed by a marriage ceremony. However, marriages in the Middle East included another step involving the parents. The father of the bride and the father of the groom would make a financial arrangement where the groom's father would pay a dowry. Then came the betrothal stage—when the man and woman were espoused to one another. It's not like being engaged in America, where either party can break the engagement. Betrothal was much more binding. The bride and groom do not live together during the betrothal, and the marriage is not physically consummated.

Joseph and Mary were espoused before Mary gave birth to Jesus. When he found out Mary was pregnant, Joseph considered divorcing Mary (although they weren't actually married yet) because during betrothal the couple was considered legally married. In that culture, if the man or woman were unfaithful, he or she would be guilty of adultery. To break off the betrothal would require a certificate of divorce.

Betrothal is an "in-between time" for the couple, a time of anticipation and waiting. The price of the bride has already been paid. And she has been betrothed to one man. Everyone is just waiting on the ceremony.

Our marriage ceremonies in the West average around $22,000, and they're typically over in 30 minutes! However, a Jewish marriage ceremony was a long, drawn out celebration. After the betrothal, the groom usually went back to his father's house where he would prepare a place for him and his bride to live. Then, when their new place was ready, he would come for his bride. It almost became a game because the bride never knew what day would be "the day." She knew the general period of time, but not the day nor the hour when her bridegroom would come for her.

As part of the tradition, the groom tried to sneak up on the bride and surprise her when she wasn't expecting it. So, she had to stay ready to go with her groom at a moment's notice. It also became a game among their friends—the groom's friends wanted to catch her off guard. It was the groomsmen's job to go ahead of the groom and shout, "Behold! The bridegroom comes!" The bride's attendants tried to stay a step ahead of them and make sure the bride was ready. This is the backdrop of Jesus' parable in Matthew 25 about the ten bridesmaids waiting for the groom to appear.

When the groom finally came for his bride, he would take her back to his father's house and the place he prepared for her, marking the official start of the marriage celebration with dancing and eating.

A Spiritual Parallel

There are several parallels between the Jewish wedding I've just described and our relationship with Christ as the Church, the Bride of Christ. From the foundation of the world, our heavenly Father paid the price for our souls with the precious blood of Jesus Christ. That's why Paul says in Acts 20:28 that Jesus "bought the church with his own blood." As believers, we are espoused to the Lord. That's exactly what Paul says in 2 Corinthians 11:2: "I promised you to one husband, to Christ, so that I might present you as a pure virgin to him."

What has Jesus been doing all this time since he ascended into heaven after his resurrection? The same thing a Jewish groom does. He said, "In my Father's house are many rooms; if it were not so, I would have told you. I am going there to prepare a place for you. And if I go and prepare a place for you, I will come back and take you to be with me that you also may be where I am" (John 14:2). The Bible says the return of Christ will be accompanied by a shout of the archangel. We don't know for sure what this angel will shout, but don't be surprised if it is, "Behold! The Bridegroom comes!"

At an American wedding, the father of the bride walks down the aisle and presents the bride to the groom. Who will present the Church to Jesus? Ephesians 5:25-27 says Jesus will present the Bride to himself. "Husbands, love your wives, just as Christ loved the church and gave himself up for her to make her holy, cleansing her by the washing with water through the word, *and to present her to himself...*" He is God the Father, God the Son and God the Holy Spirit who will present us as "a radiant church without stain or wrinkle or any other blemish, but holy and blameless."

A Reservation at the Wedding Banquet

After the wedding, we will celebrate at the "wedding supper of the Lamb" (Revelation 19:9). C. S. Lewis explained how he imagined a vision of Hell where people were seated at a giant banquet table. There were piles of food on the center of the table, but no one could raise their hand to their mouth because their arms were tied to the person sitting on either side of them. Thus, their attempts to feed themselves on the sumptuous meal resulted in an eternity of frustration and selfishness. However, the scene was much different in heaven. In heaven, he envisioned the table likewise filled with food, and everyone had a long fork, too long to feed themselves. In an act of selflessness, each person was using their long fork to lovingly feed the person across the table! Of course, this was only Lewis' imagination, but the contrast could not be more evident between the self-centered misery of those in Hell and the joyous celebration of those at the wedding feast in heaven.

Two-Word Summary of Revelation

As John sees this vision of this wedding in heaven, it's so incredible that he falls down at the feet of this angel and begins to worship the angel. The angel immediately admonishes him and says, "Worship God!" That's a perfect two-word summary of the whole book of Revelation.

Then the angel says, "…for the testimony of Jesus is the spirit of prophecy" (19:10). There are a lot of people who are really into prophecy for the wrong reasons. They analyze every prophetic nuance in the Bible trying to read between every line to determine exactly how these events are going to play out. However, if you miss Jesus in Revelation, you have missed the message of the whole Revelation! As I said at the beginning, this book of the Bible is not the revelation of the future; it is the revelation of Jesus Christ. If you don't fall more in love with Jesus as a result of studying Revelation, you have missed the whole point!

The Hero Appears

Here, at the climax of the story in Revelation 19:11, Jesus

appears on a white horse to ride into battle. When he was on earth, you'll recall he rode a lowly donkey into the city of Jerusalem. No one would have guessed then that the rider on the donkey was the King of Kings. However, at the end of Revelation, he is now seated on a magnificent steed as a conquering hero, ready to judge and make war against evil.

> I saw heaven standing open and there before me was a white horse, whose rider is called Faithful and True. With justice he judges and makes war. His eyes are like blazing fire, and on his head are many crowns. He has a name written on him that no one knows but he himself. He is dressed in a robe dipped in blood, and his name is the Word of God. (Revelation 19:11-13)

Once again, Jesus' eyes are ablaze, as they were in chapter 1. He is dressed in a robe that has been dipped in blood. The word John uses is *baptizo*, which means "to dip." This is one of the places that word is translated correctly instead of transliterated. It's a beautiful white robe, yet the corner of that robe has been dipped in blood as a reminder of the blood he shed on the cross.

At first, John does not call Jesus by name in this description. Without a doubt, however, the One on this horse is the resurrected, ascended, glorified Lord Jesus Christ for on his robe and on his thigh he has this name written: KING OF KINGS AND LORD OF LORDS (19:16).

Notice the titles John ascribes to Jesus in this passage. First, in contrast to the Antichrist and the devil, Jesus is "Faithful and True" (19:11). Can you recall a time in your life when Jesus has been untrue? Can you remember a time when he was not faithful in his promise? No, the very nature of Jesus Christ is to be worthy of trust.

John indicates Jesus also has a "name written on him known only to himself" (19:12). What is that name? When you get to heaven, you'll have your opportunity to ask Jesus because no one knows except him!

Another name describing Jesus in this passage is "The Word of God" (19:13). In Greek, it is the little phrase, "Tu logos, tu Thea": *the Logos, the Word of God.* This is how John first described Jesus in John 1:1, 14 where it says, "In the beginning was the Word [*logos*] and the Word was with God and the Word was God…the Word became flesh and made his dwelling among us." We use the spoken or written word to make thoughts and concepts more tangible. When people feel a certain way, they try to "put into words" the emotions they are experiencing. You've heard people say they "can't find the right word" to say what they mean sometimes. A word helps give expression to something that's difficult to understand. To many people, the concept of God—an almighty, spiritual being that we cannot see—is difficult to comprehend. That's why God "put himself into words" by sending Jesus to earth in human form. You want to know what God is like in one word? The word you should be thinking of is "Jesus." When you know Jesus, you know all there is to know about God himself.

The Armies of the King

Behind their Commander General, the armies of heaven follow. Note that John says the army is plural—that's intentional because there are at least two parts to this army. One is an army of angels. In Matthew 25:31, all of his angels will be with him—and don't picture sweet, chubby-cheeked cherubs. Artists have caricatured angels that way, but the Bible says the angels are powerful warriors.

In formation with the angelic army there will also be the army of saints. In the opening chapters of Revelation, we are represented by the 24 elders around the throne. In chapter 19, we are symbolized as the Bride of Christ, the Church, at a heavenly wedding and celebration. Now, we are part of an army, riding to victory with our Commander-in Chief.

The distinctive element about this army is that they are wearing bright, shining linen (19:14), which is explained in 19:8 as the "righteous acts of the saints." There are two kinds of righteousness in the Bible, and clothing is a great way to understand the difference between the two. When we get dressed, there are undergarments we wear under our clothes and outer garments we wear, like a coat or sweater.

There is a great spiritual parallel in this simple analogy. When we accept Christ as Lord and Savior, we don the inner "garment" of righteousness, which is the imputed righteousness of Jesus. You are righteous not because of anything you've done but because Jesus has given you his righteousness. Over that, you wear "the righteous acts of the saints," which are the good deeds you do in the strength of the Lord to honor God and glorify him because you love him.

The One Weapon Needed at the Final Battle

Enoch, only seven generations from Adam (according to Jude 14), was one of the first to prophesy about this heavenly assembly at the end of the Tribulation. It is a parallel passage to what we read in Revelation 19. Enoch said, "See, the Lord is coming with thousands upon thousands of his holy ones to judge everyone, and to convict all the ungodly of all the ungodly acts they have done in the ungodly way, and of all the harsh words ungodly sinners have spoken against him" (Jude 14-15).

I know what some of you reading this are thinking when you read these words. You might be thinking, "I don't really enjoy fighting, so if it's all the same to Jesus, I'll stay behind and clean up the dishes from the marriage supper of the Lamb!" Who wants to confront the world's most evil army of wickedness, right?

There's actually nothing to worry about because it is going to be the world's shortest battle. You may have noticed that John doesn't say anything about the saints carrying a weapon—they won't need one.

So, if we don't have weapons with which to fight, how are we going to win this battle? John assures us only one weapon is needed. In Revelation 19:15-16 he writes, "Out of his mouth comes a sharp sword with which to strike down the nations. He will rule them with an iron scepter. He treads the winepress of the fury of the wrath of God Almighty. On his robe and on his thigh he has this name written: KING OF KINGS AND LORD OF LORDS."

King Jesus does not wield a sword in his right hand—it's in his mouth. Hebrews 4:12 says, "For the word of God is living and active. Sharper than any double-edged sword, it penetrates even to dividing soul and spirit, joints and marrow; it judges the thoughts and attitudes of the heart." When Jesus speaks, his authority flashes like the glint of a sword. During his earthly ministry, Jesus only had to speak in order to cast out demons. Even the waves on a raging sea became instantly calm at his voice.

One of my favorite stories in the Bible is in John 18 when Jesus was in the Garden of Gethsemane with his disciples the night before he was crucified. The darkness made it difficult for the detachment of Roman soldiers to see which man was Jesus. Jesus asked them who they were looking for, and they replied, "Jesus of Nazareth." Then Jesus said, "I am he." When he spoke those simple words, the big, burly soldiers were knocked off their feet and fell to the ground!

The Bible prophesied the Messiah would wield unprecedented authority in his words. Isaiah the prophet wrote, "He will strike the earth with the rod of his mouth; with the breath of his lips he will slay the wicked!" (Isaiah 11:4). At the sound of Jesus' voice, the Final Battle of the end times will be over.

The King's Enemies

Who will oppose King Jesus at this Final Battle? Revelation 19 identifies them as kings, generals and "mighty men." They all gather to make war against the rider on the white horse, but the odds are not in their favor and the victor is already preparing to take the spoils. John says:

> And I saw an angel standing in the sun, who cried in a loud voice to all the birds flying in midair, "Come, gather together for the great supper of God, so that you may eat the flesh of kings, generals and mighty men, of horses and their riders, and the flesh of all people, free and slave, small and great." Then I saw the beast and the kings of the earth and their armies gathered together to make war against the rider on the horse and his army (Revelation 19:17-19).

Why would the nations try to overthrow God? What sort of incredible vanity would make them believe they could do it? The Psalmist wondered the same thing. In Psalm 2 he describes this very scene from Revelation 19. He writes, "The kings of the earth take their stand and the rulers gather together against the LORD and against his Anointed One." Then he asks, "Why do the nations conspire and the people plot in vain?" The answer is because Satan is motivating this army of the Antichrist. The Antichrist is Satan in the flesh, just as Jesus was God in the flesh. Satan is going to literally possess this Antichrist in his final attempt to overthrow God. You've seen black-and-white reels of Hitler rallying thousands of Nazi troops to accomplish his despicable plans. Likewise, Satan will stir up the rulers of every nation through the person of the Antichrist and convince them to attack Israel and ultimately overthrow God himself.

This is the scene as the nations gather at Armageddon (Har-Megiddo) to plot their final surge into Israel. Picture every evil ruler you can imagine throughout recorded history assembled with their armies and ready to strike: every Kim John Il, every Saddam Hussein, every Joseph Stalin, every Adolph Hitler, every Genghis Khan and so on throughout history. It's going to be the worst of the worst assembled on that plain—pure evil incarnate.

How does God react? Psalm 2:4 says, "The One enthroned in heaven laughs; the Lord scoffs at them. Then he rebukes them in his anger and terrifies them in his wrath saying, 'I have installed my King on Zion, my holy hill.'"

The Battle Begins

The quickest knockout in the early 20th century, including the full 10-count from the referee, was a welterweight fight from 1946 when Al Couture knocked out Ralph Walton in 10.5 seconds. The victor at this battle won't take that long. They won't win with a last-second shot at the buzzer! It's not going to go into double overtime. The devil and his cronies are doomed from the start. Before his very eyes, John sees the battle unfold:

> But the beast was captured, and with him the false prophet who had performed the miraculous signs on his behalf. With these signs he had deluded those who had received the mark of the beast and worshiped his image. The two of them were thrown alive into the fiery lake of burning sulfur. The rest of them were killed with the sword that came out of the mouth of the rider on the horse, and all the birds gorged themselves on their flesh. (Revelation 19:20-21)

The outcome of this battle reminds me of a time when I was in the Crimea. A pastor at Yalta showed me a cartoon out of their local paper from years earlier about the arrogant, godless attitude of atheistic communism. In the cartoon, Stalin is climbing a ladder toward heaven. At the base of the ladder were the ruins of a broken-down church building. The pastor translated the caption that said, "Having destroyed this 'god business' here on earth, we are going to destroy it in heaven." That was the attitude of Stalin and communism. I had to smile as I drove through Moscow post-communism and saw on a pedestal (where before there had been a statue of Joseph Stalin) that the statue had been removed and in its place was a cross.

The Earthly Reign of Christ

Immediately after this victory, Jesus Christ is going to set up a kingdom on earth. It will last for one thousand years—a millennium—and believers will reign with him on the earth.

CHAPTER 20

An Earthly Reign

I remember driving down a little country road one time and seeing an old clapboard church with a huge sign of their name and three words underneath: "Fundamental, Premillennial, Dispensational." The sign was almost as large as the church building! Most people don't even know what *premillennial* means. The word comes from two Latin words *mille* meaning "one thousand" and *annum* meaning "years." Millennium, therefore, means "a period of one thousand years." That little church was trying to convey on their sign their position on *when* the Lord Jesus is going to reign on the earth for one thousand years. And there are a lot of opinions on that subject.

Three Views of Eschatology

The word *eschatology* is the technical word for the study of final events. It comes from the Greek word *eschaton,* which means "last." Those who study prophecy want to know what's going to happen in the last days. The study of eschatology has led to a variety of opinions about the future. Let's look at three basic perspectives.

Amillennial

The letter "a" in front of a word cancels that word out; it's a negative. For instance, the word *muse* means "to think."

Therefore, the word *amuse* means "not thinking." That's my favorite kind of movie—something amusing so I don't have to think too hard! An *amillennialist* is someone who believes the millennial reign of Christ is figurative, not literal.

Postmillennial

The second position, which was popular at the beginning of the 20th century, is called *postmillennial.* The word *post* means "after." They believe that Jesus will return to earth after a peaceful thousand-year Golden Age where there will be no more war. In other words, they believe God is going to work through Christian men and women to help us reach our potential and bring out the best in humanity.

At the turn of the 20th century, our society was advancing technologically at a rapid rate with the introduction of steel manufacturing and the invention of the telephone, airplane and Henry Ford's mass-produced automobile—impressive new developments that showed off the sheer genius of humanity's accomplishments. Society arrogantly believed they were moving toward a social Utopia. But then came two bloody World Wars, crushing any hope for that dream. Today, few are willing to believe that society is getting progressively better when crime and violence are at all-time highs worldwide. Our conditions don't seem to be improving; instead we're witnessing the decay of goodness and decency all around us.

Premillennial

The premillennial stance holds that Jesus Christ is going to return *before* he establishes his earthly kingdom for a thousand years. I hold to this view. However, I also believe that when it comes to the details of eschatology, one can't be absolutely dogmatic. I can love and fellowship with somebody who is an amillennialist or somebody who is a postmillennialist as long as they believe in the literal return of Christ.

The Bible is totally infallible, without error, but my interpretation of it and another person's interpretation of it certainly is not. Having studied Scripture for many years, I am personally convinced of the premillennial view, as are some other premillennialists including Billy Graham, Chuck Swindoll and Dwight L. Moody. Some people look at all these views and say, "Hey, I'm *pro*-millennial." Meaning, they are in favor of Jesus ruling and reigning, period! I'm for that, too! Others jokingly say, "I'm *pan*-millennial." Meaning, it will all just "pan out" in the end.

At this point in our story, the beast and false prophet have been burned alive in the lake of burning sulphur. But what about Satan?

Satan's Prison Sentence

Satan is sentenced to spend one thousand years in the Abyss, which ushers in this wonderful time of peace called the Millennium. There's no more beast, no more false prophet and, for an extended period of time, there is no devil to contend with anymore. John writes about Satan's removal:

> And I saw an angel coming down out of heaven, having the key to the Abyss and holding in his hand a great chain. He seized the dragon, that ancient serpent, who is the devil, or Satan, and bound him for a thousand years. He threw him into the Abyss, and locked and sealed it over him, to keep him from deceiving the nations anymore until the thousand years were ended. After that, he must be set free for a short time. (Revelation 20:1-3)

Christians can make two mistakes about the devil. We can underestimate his power and think he has no influence over our lives. That's a mistake. However, an equally troubling mistake is to *over*estimate the devil and give him too much attention. Jesus told his disciples that he gave them authority over the power of the devil (Matthew 10:1). Jesus was essentially saying, "I give you *exousia* (authority) over the *dunamis* (power) of the evil one." Every believer has authority over Satan in the name of Jesus—right now.

Think about it this way. Let's say a State Trooper is standing on the side of the highway ready to pull over a speeding 18-wheeler coming right at him. Who is more powerful at that moment, the State Trooper or the semi-truck that outweighs him by thousands of pounds? The semi is more powerful. Head-to-head, the Trooper is going to get flattened.

However, suddenly this Trooper holds up his hand and says, "Stop in the name of the law!" What is that truck going to do? It's going to stop! That State Trooper is not depending on his intellectual power, his financial power or his physical power; he is standing in the authority given him by the state government, and the truck must obey.

I'm not any more powerful than Satan. In fact, I'm a lot less powerful than Satan (and so are you). However, in the name of Jesus we have authority over him! Comedian Flip Wilson would often quip about his bad behavior, "The devil made me do it!" In reality, the devil can't make a Christian do anything. He is a defeated foe. And one day he's going to be thrown into the Abyss for one thousand years.

The Rule of Christ on Earth

The worldwide reign of Christ on the earth is going to happen during the thousand years that the devil is in the Abyss. John wrote about what this millennial rule of Christ will be like:

> I saw thrones on which were seated those who had been given authority to judge. And I saw the souls of those who had been beheaded because of their testimony for Jesus and because of the word of God. They had not worshiped the beast or his image and had not received his mark on their foreheads or their hands. They came to life and reigned with Christ a thousand years. (The rest of the dead did not come to life until the thousand years were ended.) This is the first resurrection. Blessed and holy are those who have part in the first resurrection. The second death has no power over them, but they will be priests of God and of Christ and will reign with him for a thousand years. (Revelation 20:4-6)

There is a thousand-year gap between verse 6 and verse 7 when the devil is released from the Abyss. We don't know many details about the Millennium from Revelation, but there are several additional passages in the Bible that describe it, including Zechariah 14 and Isaiah 2, 11. Although the popular phrase "the lion will lie down with the lamb" isn't in the Bible, Isaiah 11:6-8 makes several contrasts between animals who are natural enemies that are now able to exist side-by-side in peace during this time—wolves and lambs, leopards and young goats. In the Millennium, nations who were former enemies will be friends.

The prophets Isaiah and Micah also predicted this time period. "Many people will come and say, 'Come let us go up to the mountain of the Lord, to the house of the God of

Jacob...He will judge between the nations...they will beat their swords into plowshares and their spears into pruning hooks. Nation will not take up sword against nation, nor will they train for war anymore" (Isaiah 2:3-4). These prophecies and others are fulfilled during the thousand-year reign of Christ on the earth.

Reigning with Christ

What's our role during this time of unparalleled peace? Revelation 20:6 promises, "We will reign with him for a thousand years." When Jesus comes to rapture the Church, he's coming *for* the saints, and we'll be caught up into the heavens. When Jesus comes at the Final Battle, he's coming *with* the saints who are part of a heavenly army. Then, after he is victorious at the Final Battle, we're going to reign with Christ a thousand years on the earth.

You may recall earlier in Revelation 1:6 where it says Jesus "has made us to be a kingdom and priests [actually it says a kingdom *of* priests] to serve his God and Father—to him be glory and power for ever and ever!" Here, John is trying to tell us a little about where this story is going before he gets to the end! "Listen up Church," he seems to be saying. "You will reign with Christ on earth one day."

Many other passages in the New Testament describe us reigning with Christ at this time. For example, 1 Corinthians 6:1-2 advises Christians not to take each other to a secular court of law instead of letting godly, objective Christians weigh in on the case since one day Christians will judge and rule the whole earth. Paul writes, "Do you not know that the saints will judge the world? And if you are to judge the world, are you not competent to judge trivial cases?" He also writes in 2 Timothy 2:12, "If we endure, we will also reign with him."

At Christmas, we sing these beautiful lyrics, "He rules the world with truth and grace and makes the nations prove the glories of his righteousness and wonders of his love." That hasn't happened yet on the earth, but the next time you sing it, be sure to smile as you know that one day Christ *will* rule on the earth, and we'll reign with him!

Saints and Humans

During the Millennium, we're going to be a kingdom of priests to judge the world and rule with Christ. A priest speaks to God on behalf of the people...and a priest speaks to people on behalf of God. We will serve a whole population of people on the earth who will be alive when Jesus wins the Final Battle.

Of course, we're going to be in our resurrected bodies, which are eternal. So how can we relate to people who are merely "human"? We will relate to others just as Jesus did. The Bible says, "But we know that when he appears, we shall be like him, for we shall see him as he is" (1 John 3:2). After Jesus was resurrected, he met with the disciples in the Upper Room and asked them to touch him. "Does a ghost have flesh and blood?" he asked. He even fixed breakfast on the shore of Galilee and ate with them—all in his resurrected body.

Three Parts of the First Resurrection

When John describes the believers who will rule with Christ, he identifies them as having been part of the "first resurrection (20:6). Paul explained this also in 1 Corinthians 15:22-25 when he wrote, "For as in Adam all die, so in Christ all will be made alive. But each in his own turn: Christ, the firstfruits; then, when he comes, those who belong to him. Then the end will come [literally, "then the end ones"], when he hands over the kingdom to God the Father after he has destroyed all dominion, authority and power. For he must reign until he has put all his enemies under his feet."

In this passage, "the end" should be translated *the end ones*; it's in the neutral gender which means *the end ones*, not the end of time. When comparing those words of Paul with John's mention of the first resurrection, we see there are three parts or groups in the "first resurrection."

1. Christ

Christ was raised from the dead 2,000 years ago. His resurrection is called the "firstfruits." That term means little to us because we aren't familiar with the Jewish festivals. It's an agricultural reference to the first bundle of wheat and barley gathered as a sacrifice of thanks to the Lord. Ancient farmers went to the Temple and waved that bundle of "firstfruits" before the Lord in appreciation for the harvest yet to come. They were thankful by faith because the rest of the field had not developed yet. When Jesus was resurrected, he was like the "firstfruits" of the resurrection and a foreshadowing of all the other believers who will come after him one day.

2. The Rapture

The next group Paul mentions is "those who belong to him." This speaks of the time when Jesus returns in the clouds to rapture the Church. The dead in Christ will rise first; then the believers who are still alive at that time will be changed in an instant into their resurrection bodies. Following the agricultural metaphor, if Christ represents the firstfruits, the Church comprises the main harvest.

What happens to a Christian the moment he or she dies? Many people have questions about this. The Bible assures us that the soul and spirit of a believer are immediately in the presence of Jesus. The body is then buried, cremated or otherwise destroyed. The Bible explains the miraculous transformation that will then happen one day when Jesus comes back to rapture the Church.

> Brothers, we do not want you to be ignorant about those who fall asleep, or to grieve like the rest of men, who have no hope. We believe that Jesus died and rose again and so we believe that God will bring with Jesus those who have fallen asleep in him. According to the Lord's own word, we tell you that we who are still alive, who are left till the coming of the Lord, will certainly not precede those who have fallen asleep. For the Lord himself will come down from heaven, with a loud command, with the voice of the archangel and with the trumpet call of God, and the dead in Christ will rise first. After that, we who are still alive and are left will be caught up together with them in the clouds to meet the Lord in the air. And so we will be with the Lord forever. (1 Thessalonians 4:13-17)

If you have lost a loved one who believed in Jesus, these should be encouraging words. They'll be the very first ones reunited with their resurrection body. Then, if we are still alive when Jesus raptures the Church, our earthly bodies will also be transformed into resurrection bodies.

3. Tribulation Saints

The third part of the first resurrection includes the

Tribulation saints. They are the "end ones." Following our harvesting metaphor, these last ones are a picture of "the gleaning" of a field. After the main harvest, there were usually several stalks of grain left in the corners of the field. Beggars always followed the harvesters to collect these leftovers.

Notice Revelation 20:6 says of all the believers who are raised in the first resurrection, "The second death has no power over them." What is the second death? Revelation 20:14 answers that question, "Then death and Hades were thrown into the lake of fire. The lake of fire is the second death," which is the place of Hell originally constructed for the devil and all his angels. The first death is physical death; the second death is eternal spiritual death. Have you noticed that people today are afraid of the first death? People do everything they can to deny the fact that death is coming. We need to be more concerned with the second death than we are the first death. Jesus said, "Do not be afraid of those who kill the body but cannot kill the soul. Rather, be afraid of the One who can destroy both soul and body in hell" (Matthew 10:28).

If you are a Christian when Jesus comes back to rapture the Church, you're part of the first resurrection. You are blessed because the second death has no power over you!

The Release of Satan

One event signals the end of the thousand years. Satan is released from captivity.

> When the thousand years are over, Satan will be released from his prison and will go out to deceive the nations in the four corners of the earth—Gog and

> Magog—to gather them for battle. In number they are like the sands on the seashore. They marched across the breadth of the earth and surrounded the camp of God's people, the city he loves. But fire came down from heaven and devoured them. And the devil, who deceived them, was thrown into the lake of burning sulfur, where the beast and the false prophet had been thrown. They'll be tormented day and night for ever and ever. (Revelation 20:7-10)

At the end of a thousand years, Satan will be released from his prison, but he still carries the sure sentence of death. He assembles the nations (symbolically referenced as Gog and Magog) against God once again for a final attempt at overthrowing God. Amazingly, even though the world will experience a perfect environment during the earthly reign of Christ, the hearts of some will grow cold once more. Following the pattern begun in the Garden of Eden, there will still be those who abandon the goodness of God to follow Satan's schemes.

In our finite minds, we don't understand why God wouldn't just do away with Satan altogether the first time when he is bound for one thousand years. What's the point of letting him out again to terrify the earth? I don't know. But perhaps one reason why God allows Satan to reappear is to prove once again the futility of human virtue. Even in a perfect environment of utter tranquility, the human heart proves to be "desperately wicked" as Jeremiah says.

Considering the prominence his part takes up throughout Revelation, Satan's final exit from the storyline is quite brief. First, fire comes down from heaven and devours his armies that were assembled against Jerusalem. Then Satan himself is thrown into the "lake of burning sulphur" (20:10) to join his cohorts, the beast and the false prophet. There, "they will be tormented day and night for ever and ever."

Final Judgment

> Then I saw a great white throne and him who was seated on it. Earth and sky fled from his presence, and there was no place for them. And I saw the dead, great and small, standing before the throne, and the books [plural] were opened. Another book was opened, which is the book of life. The dead were judged according to what they had done as recorded in the books. The sea gave up the dead that were in it, and death [which literally means "the grave"] and Hades gave up the dead that were in them, and each person was judged according to what he had done. Then death and Hades were thrown into the lake of fire. The lake of fire is the second death. If anyone's name was not found written in the book of life, he was thrown into the lake of fire. (Revelation 20:11-15)

After Satan is permanently destroyed in the lake of fire, God turns his judicial attention on the earth. This is often called the Great White Throne Judgment because of the awesome royal throne John describes as a central feature of this scene (20:11). Gathered before the throne are millions upon millions of the souls of lost people throughout the ages.

When John says, "And I saw the dead," he doesn't mean those who were physically dead. The word, *nekros*, where we get our word *necrology* speaks of those who are physically dead. However, John uses the word *thanatos*, which means spiritually dead or "lost" people. This is the second resurrection of the dead, and it is for all those who never accepted Christ as Lord and Savior.

But What About Believers?

There will be no Christians at the Great White Throne Judgment. All the believers have already participated in the first resurrection a thousand years earlier. One thousand years *later* this second resurrection of the rest of the dead (the unrighteous) takes place, as John explains in 20:5. So, who is seated on the throne to judge all of these people?

In John 5:22, Jesus said, "The Father judges no one, but has entrusted all judgment to the Son." Jesus Christ is going to be the presiding Judge. At the end of your life on earth, Jesus is either going to be your defense attorney or he's going to be your judge. In other words, he is going to be your advocate who stands before the Father and successfully pleads your case. Or you will stand before him as the Judge of all the earth. You will meet him face-to-face someday, one way or the other.

Those Who Are Judged

What happens to a lost person at the point of their physical death is very different from a Christian's experience. The body goes into the grave (dies). The Old Testament used the word *sheol* to describe where their soul and their spirit immediately goes, which is into Hades. Hades is like the county jail before the final sentencing to the state penitentiary (Hell). Interestingly, the King James Version never distinguishes between Hell and Hades. However, there are actually two different Greek words used in the Bible. One word is *gehenna,* meaning "Hell" (which I described earlier). It is the final destination of the unsaved after the Great White Throne Judgment. The other word is *Aides*, which is actually transliterated into English as Hades. In Luke 16, Jesus talked about the rich man who died and woke up in Hades. We know Hades is also a place of punishment because the rich man cried out to Abraham and said, "I am in agony in this fire" (Luke 16:24).

In Revelation 20:13, it is time for judgment, so Hades delivers up all the long-departed souls and spirits there. John said he saw all the dead assembled in heaven before God's throne, the "great and small" (20:12). Some of the biggest criminal minds and wicked rulers throughout history will be there to await judgment.

However, standing alongside are also the people who never "got around" to accepting Christ as Savior. There will be people there who coached Little League and never cheated on their taxes; they just never believed in Jesus Christ. And there will even be some church members there who thought they were saved because they went to church! Jesus said in Matthew 7:21-23, "Not everyone who says to me, 'Lord, Lord,' will enter the kingdom of heaven, but only he who does the will of my Father who is in heaven. Many will say to me on the day, 'Lord, Lord, did we not prophesy in your name, and in your name drive out demons and perform many miracles?' Then I will tell them plainly, 'I never knew you. Away from me, you evildoers!'"

The most disturbing word in this passage is the word, "many…". It's not just a few who will be surprised to find their good deeds did not earn them a spot in heaven; the Bible says "many." There is an eternity of difference between practicing religion and having a personal relationship with Jesus Christ.

The Books in Heaven

John sees some books are opened at this Great White Throne Judgment. We're not told how many books will be there, but I believe one of the open books on that day will be the Bible. It is God's holy standard for all of humanity and his love letter of grace through Jesus Christ. It is the Book of Law.

There will also be the Book of Works because it says the dead "were judged according to what they had done, as recorded in the books" (20:12). The standard of God's Law requires perfect obedience. If one of the dead people were found to have kept the Law perfectly throughout his or her lifetime, I suppose that person could be admitted into heaven that day. However, the Bible says perfection is impossible because of our sinful nature. In fact, only Jesus Christ perfectly fulfilled God's Law by never having a selfish, sinful thought and never committing a sinful act. Therefore, God laid on him, the perfect sacrifice, the punishment for everyone's sin—which is death.

However, those who do not personally acknowledge and accept Jesus Christ's sacrifice will have only their own good works to point to on that day. And sadly, the few lines or even a few pages of good works over their lifetime doesn't begin to meet God's standard in God's open book, the Book of Law.

The most important book that will be there is the Book of Life. John says, "If anyone's name was not found written in the book of life, he was thrown into the lake of fire" (20:15). Earlier in Revelation 3, Jesus mentioned this Book of Life when he addressed the church at Sardis, foreshadowing this end-of-time event at the Great White Throne Judgment. As the reward for being faithful Jesus says, "I will never blot out his name from the book of life, but will acknowledge his name before my Father and his angels."

Some who believe you can be saved and then lose your salvation point to this passage as evidence to support their position. They say, "If it is not possible to lose your salvation, why does the Bible say Jesus will blot some names out of the

Book of Life?" That's a misunderstanding of this verse. The Bible says, "God is not willing that any should perish, but that all should come to repentance" (2 Peter 3:9).

There is a Book of Life in heaven, and everyone whose name is in there will be saved, but nowhere in the Bible does it use the verb describing God "writing down" the names in the book. Some scholars suggest that everybody's name is written in the Lamb's Book of Life from the foundation of the world, and it is only when a person commits the blasphemy against the Holy Spirit by ultimately and finally rejecting Jesus that their names are blotted out.

Have you ever gone on a trip and your hotel could not find your reservation? It is a desolate feeling to have made a trip and suddenly realize you might not have a place to stay. There is one reservation you need to be absolutely certain you have confirmed, and it is your reservation in heaven. Do you know what your confirmation number is? Write this down—it's John 3:16. It says, "For God so loved the world that he gave his one and only Son that whoever believes in him shall not perish but have eternal life." God did everything he could for as many as possible to avoid this fate on that day. He gave his Son so that your name would never be blotted out from the Book of Life. What is your response to him?

CHAPTER 21

The New Jerusalem

I remember asking a children's Sunday school class one time, "How many of you boys and girls want to go to heaven?" Every child except one little boy raised their hand. Perplexed by his answer, I smiled and said, "You mean you don't want to go to heaven?" He answered with utter seriousness, "Well, my mother said we had to come straight home after church." In Revelation 21:1-5, John writes about what Christians will experience when they arrive in heaven:

> Then I saw a new heaven and a new earth, for the first heaven and the first earth had passed away, and there was no longer any sea. I saw the Holy City, the new Jerusalem, coming down out of heaven from God, prepared as a bride beautifully dressed for her husband. And I heard a loud voice from the throne saying, "Now the dwelling of God is with men, and he will live with them. They will be his people, and God himself will be with them and be their God. He will wipe every tear from their eyes. There will be no more death or mourning or crying or pain, for the old order of things has passed away." He who was seated on the throne said, "I am making everything new!" Then he said, "Write this down, for these words are trustworthy and true."

Heaven Can Wait?

The New Jerusalem is depicted as the "capital city" of the eternal kingdom of God. But it's not all there is to the new heaven and the new earth. In Scripture, the word "heaven" is used to describe three distinct elements. There is the first heaven, which speaks of the atmosphere (the sky). The second use of the word means "cosmic space," as in Psalm 8:3 where the Bible says, "When I consider the heavens, the work of your fingers, the moon and the stars, which you have set in place…" The third use of the word "heaven" is the dwelling place of God. In 2 Corinthians 12:2, Paul says "a man in Christ" (whom I believe was Paul) was "caught up to the third heaven," the dwelling place of God. Like John, Paul was given a supernatural vision of heaven. Paul was so enamored by what he saw that God gave him a thorn in the flesh to keep him humble. No wonder Paul wrote in Philippians 1:21-24 about how difficult it was to remain patient despite his overwhelming desire to be in heaven with Jesus. He'd seen it firsthand! Let your mind start thinking about the glory of heaven and you will feel conflicted like Paul—wanting to go, but waiting on God's timing. Jesus said in John 14:2, "In my Father's house are many rooms; if it were not so, I would have told you. I am going there to prepare a place for you." Most homes today are built within six to twelve months. Jesus, the Master Carpenter, has been in heaven preparing a place for his followers for over 2000 years. What will that place be like?

What's *Not* in Heaven

I love the things that *aren't* going to be in heaven as much as what *will* be there. There will be no more tears, mourning or pain, according to Revelation 21:4. Physical and emotional pain is part of our everyday existence on earth. Some people live with constant physical pain that is almost debilitating. Many live with lifelong emotional pain from depression, rejection and personal trials. In heaven, there is nothing like that anymore. And there will be no more death. The first death in the Bible occurred when Cain murdered his brother, Abel. Since that time, there has been a long funeral procession of every human who has ever lived. In heaven, there will be no funeral homes, no obituaries and no cemeteries.

The Bible also tells us *who* will *not* be in heaven. John lists them in Revelation 20:8: "...the cowardly, the unbelieving, the vile, the murderers, the sexually immoral, those who practice magical arts, the idolaters and all liars." The list continues in verse 27 of that same chapter: "Nothing impure will ever enter it, nor will anyone who does what is shameful or deceitful, but only those whose names are written in the Lamb's book of life." You probably would never walk alone, especially at night, through a major crime center. Why? Evil people: criminals, drug addicts, rapists, robbers and thieves rule the night there. However, not so in heaven! There won't be anybody like that to fear!

The New Jerusalem

John goes into minute detail when describing a personal tour he received of the New Jerusalem:

> One of the seven angels who had the seven bowls full of the seven last plagues came and said to me, "Come, I will show you the bride, the wife of the Lamb." And he carried me away in the Spirit to a mountain great and high, and showed me the Holy City, Jerusalem, coming down out of heaven from God. It shone with the glory of God, and its brilliance was like that of a very precious jewel, like a jasper, clear as crystal. It had a great, high wall with twelve gates, and with twelve angels at the gates. On the gates were

> written the names of the twelve tribes of Israel. There were three gates on the east, three on the north, three on the south and three on the west. The wall of the city had twelve foundations. (Revelation 21:9-10)

Picture this beautiful capital city. There are walls around the city with three gates on each side. There are twelve layers of foundations, each with the names of the apostles.

The angel conducting John's tour has a golden measuring rod to make sure John notes its dimensions.

> The city was laid out like a square, as long as it was wide. He measured the city with the rod and found it to be 12,000 stadia in length, and as wide and high as it is long. He measured its wall and it was 144 cubits thick, by man's measurement, which the angel was using. The wall was made of jasper, and the city of pure gold, as pure as glass. The foundations of the city walls were decorated with every kind of precious stone. The first foundation was jasper, the second sapphire, the third chalcedony, the fourth emerald, the fifth sardonyx, the sixth carnelian, the seventh chrysolite, the eighth beryl, the ninth topaz, the tenth chrysoprase, the eleventh jacinth and the twelfth amethyst. The twelve gates were twelve pearls, each gate made of a single pearl. The great street of the city was of pure gold, like transparent glass. (Revelation 21:16-21)

In this passage, you will likely recognize the popular descriptions of heaven as having "pearly gates" and "streets of gold." John is working within the limits of earthbound, human language to describe what is indescribable beauty. Earthly jewels and metals like gold and silver fall short of describing the unbelievable sight.

I once read a true story about a young boy born blind for the first ten years of his life. However, some surgeons performed an experimental operation on him to try to restore his sight. When they removed the bandages after his surgery, he looked up into the face of the doctor and his eyes gleamed with recognition. Then he looked over at his mother, who beamed with pride as her son saw her face for the first time. When he looked toward the window of his room, he asked his mom to help him up so he could stand there and look. The view from his window was simple—only a small patch of grass and a few flowers in a courtyard under a clear, blue sky. "Oh mother!" he cried. "Why didn't you tell me it was so beautiful?" Can you imagine the sensory overload he experienced? When we get to heaven, we are going to be so overwhelmed with its beauty that words will fail us.

In addition to its extraordinary beauty, heaven is exceedingly big. The measurement of 12,000 "stadia" is about 1,431 miles—that's about the distance from New York City to Miami one way. Since the city is a cube (as high and wide as it is long), you can estimate the size by multiplying 1,431 miles, by 1,431 miles, by 1,431 miles. The result is almost three billion cubic miles. That's just the capital city of the new heaven and the new earth. When God does something, he does it big!

The River of Life

I'm going to skip ahead to the first part of Chapter 22 because John continues writing about this marvelous scene in heaven. He next sees the River of Life, flowing down the middle of a great golden street running the length of the city (about 1400 miles long!).

> Then the angel showed me the river of the water of life, as clear as crystal, flowing from the throne of God and of the Lamb down the middle of the great street of the city. On each side of the river stood the tree of life, bearing twelve crops of fruit, yielding its fruit every month. And the leaves of the tree are for the healing of the nations. No longer will there be any curse. The throne of God and of the Lamb will be in the city, and his servants will serve him. They will see his face, and his name will be on their foreheads. There will be no more night. They will not need the light of a lamp or the light of the sun, for the Lord God will give them light. And they will reign forever and ever. The angel said to me, "These words are trustworthy and true. The Lord, the God of the spirits of the prophets, sent his angel to show his servants the things that must soon take place." (Revelation 22:1-6)

In the middle of "Hallelujah Avenue" is a river with crystal clear water that symbolizes nourishment, life and cleansing. Jesus said earlier in Revelation 21:6, "To him who is thirsty I will give to drink without cost from the spring of the water of life." This river has as its source the throne of God. But it is only one central feature of heaven—there is another central feature in the Master Architect's design for heaven. It is the Tree of Life.

The Tree of Life

What do you picture when you hear "the tree of life"? Do you picture one tree standing prominently in the middle of heaven? Look again at the text. Revelation 22:2 says, "…on each side of the river stood the tree of life." One tree cannot stand on both sides of the river. This passage is using the term "tree" generically, much like one might say, "The pine tree is indigenous to East Texas." We're not talking about one tree; we're talking about many trees.

On the outside of the great street running down the center of heaven are trees of life, planted at various intervals. They bear fruit every month, season after season for eternity. John also identifies the leaves of this tree as bearing marvelous qualities. They are "for the health of the nations" (22:2), which means the citizens of heaven won't grow old, tired or ill.

Seeing Jesus

What makes heaven so heavenly? It's not gates of pearl; it's not streets of gold; it's not a tree; it's not even a river. Those things are all amazing—but there is one dominant feature of heaven that makes it the glorious city that it is. Jesus makes heaven the most incredible place we can imagine. When you get to heaven, as great as seeing your loved ones will be, the first One you will see is Jesus. And you may decide to spend the first two or three billion years of eternity at his feet just saying, "Thank you, Jesus, for doing all this for me."

CHAPTER 22

The Last Words of Jesus

As we come to this final section of the entire Bible, I want to point out that although 40 different men wrote the Bible over a period of 1,600 years, it has only One Author. God waited until the end of his Book to reveal eight of the most important truths that we can know as Christians. These essential principles are tied to the exclusive blessing God promises those who study the book of Revelation and "take it to heart" (Revelation 1:3).

The Last Command: Worship God

There are many commands contained the Bible, but the last one is found in Revelation 22:9. John was so overwhelmed with his vision of the New Jerusalem that once again he fell down to worship at the feet of the angel who was conducting his tour. Horrified, the angel immediately told John not to do so. "Do not do it! I am a fellow servant with you and with your brothers the prophets and of all who keep the words of this book. Worship God!" (22:9).

In a sense, this final command is a good summary of all the commands of the Bible. The word "worship" means to give "worth-ship." It means to ascribe worth to something or someone. Jesus said the greatest commandment was to love the Lord with all of your being. Worship is our expression of love to God. The words of this angel remind us that we are not to worship the Bible, a preacher, a denomination, a religion or a church. We are to worship God alone. If you worship anything or anyone else, you will ultimately be disappointed.

The Last Principle: After Death, it's Too Late

The Old Testament is basically a book of commands, but the New Testament is a book of principles by which we can live. A spiritual principle is a statement of truth that requires us to apply God-given wisdom to know how to follow it. This final spiritual principle says: "Let him who does wrong continue to do wrong; let him who is vile continue to be vile; let him who does right continue to do right; and let him who is holy continue to be holy" (Revelation 22:11).

This truth addresses the misunderstanding some people have that they will have time to change after they die. I've heard more than one person say, "I can live like the devil down here if I want to, but when I get to heaven I'm going to live like an angel!"

The Bible does say that those of us who follow Jesus will be "changed" in the twinkling of an eye. However, that speaks of Christ's followers, not people who live wicked lives. If you live an unholy life now, that's the kind of character you will maintain for eternity. On the other hand, if you have walked closely with Jesus, trying to maintain a life that honors him, then when you die you will fit right in with the life we'll live in eternity in heaven. That's why Christians must encourage everyone to repent and let Jesus change them now, while there is still time. There will be no opportunity to repent after a person dies.

The Last Description of Jesus: I AM

Throughout his ministry, Jesus provided dozens of personal identifications of his character. Take a concordance and go through the New Testament to identify every time Jesus says, "I am." You'll find such great self-descriptions as, "I am the Way; I am the Truth; I am the Light; I am the Bread of Life; I am the Living Water; I am the Door." Every time Jesus said, "I am," he was revealing a little more about his character. Every good Israelite recognized that phrase, "I am," as the name God revealed to Moses at the burning bush in Exodus 3. In these final verses of the Bible, Jesus shares his last three "I am" statements. "I am the Alpha and the Omega, the First and the Last, the Beginning and the End" (Revelation 22:13). He concludes by saying, "I am the Root and the Offspring of David, and the bright Morning Star" (22:16). Even in his last words to us, Jesus shows us how much he wants us to know him personally. "This is who I am," he says to the readers of Revelation. "I want you to know me."

The Alpha and Omega

I remember in the late 1960s we sang a song called, "He's Everything to Me." I used to love that song, but as I thought about the lyrics later I realized that this song only presents a partial picture of Jesus. He is more than just everything *to me*; he is everything—period. Whether he is everything to me personally doesn't matter. He is the first and last and everything we need.

The Root and Offspring of David

According to human genealogy, Jesus was the offspring of King David. In fact, the human genealogy of Jesus, recorded in both Matthew 1 and Luke 3, confirms this fact. But Jesus made the audacious claim that he was the *root* of David. He claimed to be the predecessor of David, although he was "born" on earth generations later. That would be like me saying, "I am both the ancestor and the descendant of my father." Once again, Jesus reveals that he is God in the flesh. How could he exist before David? As eternal God, he has always existed!

On one occasion, the Pharisees were bragging to Jesus about their father, Abraham. Jesus essentially said, "Listen, guys. Before Abraham was, I am!" (John 8:58). That blew their minds! Jesus (now in his thirties on earth) was trying to tell them he was alive before Abraham (who lived 2,000 years ago)! There are members of some "Christian cults" (an oxymoron) who do not believe Jesus is equal to God the Father. The next time they knock on your door, ask them to explain this unique claim of Jesus. And when they pull out their so-called "New World Translation" of the Scriptures, you'll see that they have mistranslated that verse. They don't translate it correctly, and any knowledgeable, honest Greek scholar will tell you they mistranslated it to try to make it fit their heresy that says Jesus is not equal to God the Father. Jesus, himself, said, "Before Abraham was, I existed, and before David existed, I existed." Only Jesus can make that claim because He is, in fact, God.

The Bright Morning Star

Have you ever awakened early some morning when the air is cool and crisp and the sky is beginning to lighten? If you look toward the horizon and see one star shining, it's actually not a star at all—it's the planet, Venus. That's who Jesus is to us. When we've passed through the darkest time of life, Jesus is still shining. If you put your faith in money, other people or religion, those stars have long been extinguished. But Jesus is still there for you after the longest dark nights of your life.

The Last Blessings: Obey Me

In the Sermon on the Mount, Jesus shared what we call "beatitudes." These are the statements that start with the word, "Blessed." The Latin word for blessed, fortunate or happy is *beatus*, thus we call them "beatitudes." Like the Sermon on the Mount, there are beatitudes or blessings in Revelation, and we come to the last pair here in Revelation 22. Revelation 22:7 says, "Blessed is he who keeps the words of the prophecy in this book."

In the first chapter of Revelation, we read the first beatitude: "Blessed is he who reads the words of this prophecy and keeps them" (1:3). This is the only book in the Bible that specifically offers a blessing for those who will read it and obey it. We're blessed when we read majestic portions of Scripture like Psalms, Romans and Ephesians, but none of these books promise a specific blessing. Revelation is not a book to satisfy a reader's craving for prophecy. It is a book that reveals Jesus; as a result, it produces greater obedience in our lives.

Revelation 22:14 is the final beatitude, which says, "Blessed are those who wash their robes…" The verb "wash" is actually in the passive voice, which means it should be translated, "Blessed are those who *have had their robes washed*." A mistranslation of Revelation 22:14 in the King James Version appears as, *"Blessed are those who keep his commandments."* The translators for King James used Erasmus' Greek text called the *Textus Receptus* because it was the only one available at the time. Since the translation of the King James Bible in 1611, thousands of portions of the Greek text of the New Testament have been uncovered. Today, we have over 30,000 texts and portions of texts of the New Testament. And the best Greek texts agree that verse 14 says, "Blessed are they who have their robes washed white." Nobody goes to heaven by keeping the commandments! Titus, 3:5 says, "Not by works of righteousness which we have done, but according to his mercy, he has saved us." The only way you can go to heaven is by having your robe washed white—not in super-strength detergent—but in the blood of Jesus Christ.

The Last Invitation: Come and Drink!

In Revelation 22:17, John writes: "The Spirit and the bride say, 'Come!' And let him who hears say, 'Come!'" And then God extends this beautiful invitation: "Whoever is thirsty, let him come; and whoever wishes, let him take the free gift of the water of life." God's last invitation in the Bible is, "Come and drink of the water of life!"

I'm convinced one of God's favorite words is, "Come!" There was only one time God ever said, "Get out!" He said that to Adam and Eve after they had sinned. Ever since that time, God has been inviting men and women to come back into fellowship with him. Jesus said, "If a man is thirsty, let him come to me and drink" (John 7:37). He said, "Come to me, all you who are weary and burdened, and I will give you rest" (Matthew 11:28).

In the Old Testament, God told Noah to build an ark to

save his family from judgment. As it started to rain, Noah and all the animals were still outside the ark. In the Hebrew text, we read God literally says, "Noah, *come* into the ark!" (Genesis 7:1) He didn't point down from heaven and say, "Hey, Noah! Go get in the ark!" The picture is of God already being inside the ark itself and curving his arm toward him, saying, "*Come inside!*" It was not the ark protecting Noah and all those animals—they found shelter inside the protective presence of God.

God is extending his gracious invitation to you right now. He says, "Come to me!" Salvation is a free gift from God, and you cannot earn a gift. A gift is something given to you out of love. Sadly, there are many Americans who apply the hard-work ethic approach to faith. They come from a generation that worked hard and said, "If you want something in life, you have to work hard for it!" And sometimes those same people apply that attitude toward salvation. However, we will never earn acceptance with God through our good deeds. Salvation is a free gift that can only be humbly accepted or rejected.

Every time I read this verse, I'm reminded of something that happened to me several years ago. I once taught the entire book of Revelation in one week at a church where I was a guest speaker. When I came to this last chapter, the auditorium was packed. At this verse, I said, "God says, 'If you want to be saved, come!'" Even though I had more material to teach in order to finish Revelation 22, a young man began literally running down the aisle toward the platform. I said, "What are you doing?" He said, "I'm coming to God right now!" What faith! The church pastor then took this eager young man aside and led him to accept Christ while I finished teaching.

The Last Warning: Don't Alter the Word

Revelation 22:18 says, "I warn everyone who hears the words of the prophecy of this book: If anyone adds anything to them, God will add to him the plagues described in this book. And if anyone takes words away from this book of prophecy, God will take away from him his share in the tree of life and in the holy city, which are described in this book." This warning is applied specifically to the book of Revelation, but it is a powerful principle that applies to the entire Bible because "All scripture is inspired of God" (2 Timothy 3:16). The word, "inspired," means "God-breathed." God breathed (inspired) these words into the minds of the different men who wrote the Bible.

I also believe when God gave John the final word of Revelation that his written revelation ceased. He's still speaking to us through his Holy Spirit today, but there are no additional written words from God.

Mormons are wonderful people. I admire them for their emphasis on decency and family. And they say that they believe the Bible, but they have added The Book of Mormon to the Bible. Muslims claim to believe the Bible, but they claim that the Koran supersedes the Bible because it was given to Mohammed later than the Bible was written. Mormons and Muslims add to the Word of God.

But sometimes, ignorant Christians also "add" to the Word of God by claiming the Bible says things that it never says. You'll hear them say things like, "Well the Bible says, 'Cleanliness is next to godliness.'" Or "The Bible says, 'God helps those who help themselves.'" Neither of those statements is in the Bible! In fact, I wrote a book entitled, *"No, That's NOT in the Bible"* to address some of the most common misquotations of the Bible. So be careful that you don't add anything to the Bible.

In reality, the other side of that warning is where most of us have a problem. We tend to "take away" from God's Word by ignoring portions of it. If you've been to the home of Thomas Jefferson, one of our founding fathers, you'll see a copy of the "Jefferson Bible." Jefferson didn't believe parts of the Bible, so he literally cut them out of his Bible. What remained were some of the moral teachings of Jesus, having removed all the references to the deity of Christ and his miracles. There's not much left in the Jefferson Bible because the Bible is a book filled with miracles! You may not use a pair of scissors, but whenever you knowingly ignore the clear teaching of the Word of God, you're doing the same thing that Jefferson did. You are "taking away" from the Bible. Pay heed to God's final warning.

The Last Promise: I am Coming Soon!

I was once told that there are 365 promises in the Bible, one for every day in the year. According to the great Bible teacher, Herbert Lockyer, there are actually over 5,400 promises in the Bible, as he wrote in his book *All the Promises of the Bible*. Here in Revelation 22, we find the final promise of the Bible. These are literally the last words of Christ: "I am coming soon." Jesus repeats this promise three times in Revelation 22. In verse 7, he says, "Behold, I am coming soon." Again in verse 12, "Behold, I am coming soon." Then, in verse 20, "He who testifies to these things says, 'Yes, (meaning *certainly, without a doubt*) I am coming soon."

The first promise in the Bible is found in Genesis 2:16-17

where God said to Adam and Eve, "And the LORD God commanded the man, 'You are free to eat from any tree in the garden; but you must not eat from the tree of the knowledge of good and evil, for when you eat of it you will surely die.'" God promised that sin would be the cause of all their problems. However, Jesus' last promise erases the damage of sin because he is coming soon to set everything right again. If it was "soon" two thousand years ago when these words were written, it's much sooner now. So get ready and stay ready!

The Last Prayer: Amen, Come

The final prayer of the Bible is found in Revelation 22:20. When Jesus uttered his final promise of his pending return, John prayed, "Amen, Come, Lord Jesus." The word "amen" means "let it be." John was agreeing with Jesus, and he reinforced it by saying, "Oh, Lord Jesus, please come!"

Is that a prayer that you can pray honestly? Do you want Jesus to return right now? In 2 Timothy 4, we read some of the last recorded words of the Apostle Paul. He wrote to Timothy, "I have fought the good fight, I have finished the race, I have kept the faith. Now, there is in store for me the crown or righteousness, which the Lord, the righteous Judge will award to me on that day and not only to me, but also to all have have longed for his appearing" (2 Timothy 4:7-8). Do you long for the appearing of the Lord?

One of my earliest memories from childhood is a time when my friend and I went into another friend's open garage and started hauling off all his belongings as a practical joke. We took his bicycle, his baseball equipment—everything! We made several trips stealing his stuff and hiding it in a field between our houses. As we were making our last haul, our friend's mother drove up and caught us in the act!

My mother was so enraged by my behavior that she called my dad to come home from work and give me the appropriate punishment. I can recall waiting for my dad to appear. I was miserable. In no way was I longing for his appearing! The Bible says, "And now little children, continue in him, so that when he appears we may be confident and unashamed before him at his coming" (1 John 2:28). I was ashamed when I saw my dad face-to-face because of what I'd done.

Are there things in your life that are keeping you from truly longing for the return of the Lord? Won't you confess them and repent *now* so that you can face Jesus with confidence instead of shame? After my dad spanked me, he left me alone with my tears to consider the error of my ways. Then he came back in my room and put his arms around me. He told me he expected better of me because he loved me.

By the time you read this last page in this book, you will likely have one of two reactions. You may be sighing with relief because you know you are ready for the Lord's return at any moment. You're unafraid of the future because you know you are walking with the Lord and trying to honor him with your life. However, if you feel uneasy or fearful because you're not prepared to meet Jesus face-to-face, I have a final word for you, too. In fact, I want the last words in my book to reflect the very last words of the book of Revelation, which are about *grace*. God offers the grace of his forgiveness of every sin through the sacrifice of his Son, Jesus. May the "grace of the Lord Jesus" be with you as you seek his face and find his mercy.